THE
HUMMING
EFFECT

"At the heart of health and healing is your body's energies. At the heart of your body's energies is vibration. *The Humming Effect* teaches you how to use your capacity to hum to create vibrations that promote health, healing, and higher consciousness. This is a worthy endeavor, and the book guides you on every step of the way. Jonathan and Andi Goldman are pioneers in the healing use of sound, and you are the beneficiary!"

DONNA EDEN, AUTHOR OF *ENERGY MEDICINE*

"This magnificent book will teach you new ways of using one of the most extraordinary instruments on the planet—your vocal apparatus. With what evolution has bestowed upon you, you can become a maestro at facilitating your own health, healing, and happiness. No gadgets or expensive technology required."

DAVID FEINSTEIN, PH.D., COAUTHOR OF *THE ENERGIES OF LOVE*

"Hmmmmmmmm. So simple, yet so intricate! Jonathan and Andi Goldman have written a paramount book that reveals the science and art for why creating a humming practice is not only necessary, it's fun! Knowledge is power. However, knowledge about yourself is self-empowerment. This book reveals a conscious application for using humming to optimize the health of your mind and body. *The Humming Effect* is a gift that keeps giving. Enjoy!"

DR. DARREN R. WEISSMAN, AUTHOR OF *THE POWER OF INFINITE LOVE & GRATITUDE* AND DEVELOPER OF THE LIFELINE TECHNIQUE

"Since the time of the Indian rishis the sound of humming has been acknowledged as the fundamental vibration of our divine self. The Goldmans have superbly, practically, and with great simplicity expanded upon this truth and demonstrated the potency of the hum to heal at all levels of our being. *The Humming Effect,* with its audio tracks, is an essential text in extending the range of what the human voice can achieve in self-empowered wellness."

JAMES D'ANGELO, PH.D., AUTHOR OF
THE HEALING POWER OF THE HUMAN VOICE

"I love this book! Once I started I couldn't put it down. It serves a great purpose in giving a deep education about sound, elegantly stated in a very friendly format. For anyone interested in the profound power of sound to heal and transform their lives, I heartily recommend *The Humming Effect* by the acclaimed maestros Jonathan and Andi Goldman."

TODD OVOKAITYS, M.D.,
COAUTHOR OF *12-STRAND DNA HEALING TECHNIQUES*

"*The Humming Effect* by Jonathan and Andi Goldman is a must-read primer for anyone interested in the effects of sound on cells, the body, and health. Their elegant and direct approach weaves basic research on sound with the specific benefits of sound and humming. Through infusing this book with stories and practices, they lead the reader on an enjoyable journey into their passion for humming as a tool for health and healing."

ANN MARIE CHIASSON, M.D., AUTHOR OF *ENERGY HEALING*

"Sound—from its historical perspective, mechanisms of action, and applications for wellness— is an integral part of Jonathan and Andi Goldman's new book, *The Humming Effect.* I intend to refer my readers to this book as a valued supplement to help them further understand the healing power of sound."

GEORGE L. LINDENFELD, PH.D., NEUROPSYCHOLOGIST
AND AUTHOR OF *BRAIN ON FIRE*

"A beautiful and invaluable masterpiece in sound medicine."

RANJIE N. SINGH, PH.D., AUTHOR OF *SELF-HEALING*

HUMMING EFFECT

Sound Healing
for **Health**
and **Happiness**

Jonathan Goldman
and **Andi Goldman**

Healing Arts Press
Rochester, Vermont • Toronto, Canada

Healing Arts Press
One Park Street
Rochester, Vermont 05767
www.HealingArtsPress.com

Text stock is SFI certified

Healing Arts Press is a division of Inner Traditions International

Note to the reader: *This book is intended as an informational guide. The remedies,
approaches, and techniques described herein are meant to supplement, and not to be a
substitute for, professional medical care or treatment. They should not be used to treat
a serious ailment without prior consultation with a qualified health care professional.*

Library of Congress Cataloging-in-Publication Data
Names: Goldman, Jonathan, 1949- author. | Goldman, Andi, 1948- author.
Title: The humming effect : sound healing for health and happiness / Jonathan
    Goldman and Andi Goldman.
Description: Rochester, Vermont : Healing Arts Press, [2017] | Includes index.
Identifiers: LCCN 2016052566 (print) | LCCN 2016052663 (e-book) |
    ISBN 9781620554845 (paperback) | ISBN 9781620554852 (e-book)
Subjects: LCSH: Sound—Therapeutic use. | Mind and body. | Self-care, Health.
    | BISAC: BODY, MIND & SPIRIT / Healing / General. | SELF-HELP
    / Personal Growth / General. | BODY, MIND & SPIRIT / Inspiration &
    Personal Growth.
Classification: LCC RZ999 .G642 2017 (print) | LCC RZ999 (e-book) |
    DDC 615.8/3—dc23
LC record available at https://lccn.loc.gov/2016052566

Printed and bound in the United States by Lake Book Manufacturing, Inc.
The text stock is SFI certified. The Sustainable Forestry Initiative® program
promotes sustainable forest management.

10 9 8 7 6 5 4 3 2 1

Text design by Priscilla Baker and layout by Virginia Scott Bowman
This book was typeset in Garamond Premier Pro and Gill Sans with Colaborate
used as the display typeface

To send correspondence to the author of this book, mail a first-class letter to the
author c/o Inner Traditions • Bear & Company, One Park Street, Rochester, VT
05767, and we will forward the communication, or contact the authors directly at
www.healingsounds.com.

We dedicate this book to each other!
It has been a work of deep love, respect, and joy,
and we could not have done it without each other. With
sincere gratitude and appreciation, we humbly honor the
extraordinary relationship we have been blessed with
and which has allowed this book to manifest.

Contents

⌒

PART I
Basic Principles

PART II

Practice Makes Perfect

Foreword

Humming is an instinctive sound healing practice that begins in childhood. It is a form of toning (vocalization of elongated vowel sounds) and music making that brings inner balance. Everyone around the world hums, regardless of culture or creed. We do not question why we hum any more than we question why we breathe. We just do. However, as we will see, science is starting to catch up, offering evidence of how humming supports our health and well-being.

I cannot remember a time when I did not hum. I hummed while playing the piano in my early childhood. I would make up sound adventures and then hum them all day. When I got older, I began giving piano performances. The first time I heard a recording of one of my recitals, I was shocked to find that I had been humming along with the music—loud enough for the audience to hear me. I had not even known that I was humming.

Eventually I realized that humming was an integral part of how I learned and memorized musical compositions. When I was away from the piano, I used to practice on a folding cardboard keyboard without sound; I would hum the notes as my fingers moved over the keyboard. When I was studying piano at Indiana University, I took a master class with the concert pianist Vladimir Ashkenazy. We were sitting at a table in the student lounge waiting for the teaching room to open. He wanted to get on with the lesson and so he told me to play the first movement of Beethoven's *Tempest* Sonata on the table. He hummed as he watched my hands playing the sonata on the tabletop.

He would say things like "more feeling here" and then have me replay the passage, and we would both hum with more feeling. This went on for over half an hour, and during this time people started to gather around the table to hear the master class. When the lesson was over, everyone clapped. I told Vladimir about my stage humming and how I was trying to control it during concerts. He looked at me and there was a long silence. He hummed a long *hummmmmmmmmmmmm*. Then we got up and went home. The next evening I got a seat in the front row for his piano concert. I could hear him humming while he played.

I have been teaching students to use a tuning fork to balance their nervous system for over forty years. I have always taught them to hum with the tuning fork. I tell them that humming is just as important as the tuning fork. The tuning fork trains your nervous system to come into tonal balance. Humming in resonance with the tuning fork amplifies the balancing effect. Humming is a sonic anchor for creating a balanced state. Ultimately, you do not even need a tuning fork. You can pretend you are inside the tuning fork sound and hum instead.

Now to the science. Beginning in 2001, I worked with Cell Dynamics Labs in association with the State University of New York. The focus of our work was on a compound called nitric oxide (NO), a neural transmitter that is fundamental to our health and well-being. NO is released as a gas in six-minute cycles by endothelial, neuronal, and immune cells. A compromise in NO release is a precursor to many diseases, including heart disease, upper and lower motor neuron disease, amyotrophic lateral sclerosis (ALS), depression, Parkinson's, autoimmune diseases, Alzheimer's, digestive disorders, and sexual dysfunction.

Over the course of our research, we discovered that the sound produced by BioSonic tuning forks spiked NO release in the body. We immediately published a paper on that subject in *Medical Science Monitor*.* Not long after, I began seeing research papers on humming and NO that suggested that nasal NO levels increase greatly during humming, as compared to silent exhalation.† Suddenly, all those years that I had spent humming music and teaching my students to hum with tuning forks made sense at a whole new level.

Now Jonathan and Andi Goldman have written an entire book dedicated to the subject of humming that is full of important information and exercises. Everyone who hums—in other words, every one of us—needs to read their book and enjoy a most special humming upgrade.

Edgar Cayce was a great psychic known as the "sleeping prophet." He once said during a psychic reading, "Do attempt to bring greater harmonies into the experience through the practice and through the application of self in making music. Even though it be only on a comb . . . MAKE MUSIC!"

Knowing what we know about sound healing, nitric oxide, and humming, I would modify Cayce's reading to this: "Do attempt to bring greater harmonies into the experience through the practice and through the application of self in making music. **Even though it be only humming** . . . MAKE SOUND AND MUSIC!"

JOHN BEAULIEU, N.D., PH.D.
STONE RIDGE, NEW YORK

---

*John Beaulieu, Minsun Kim, Elliott Salamon, and George B. Stefano, "Sound Therapy Induced Relaxation: Down Regulating Stress Processes and Pathologies," *Medical Science Monitor* 9, no. 5 (2003): RA116–21.
†Eddie Weitzberg, and Jon O. N. Lundberg, "Humming Greatly Increases Nasal Nitric Oxide," *American Journal of Respiratory and Critical Care Medicine* 166, no. 2 (2002): 144–45; and Jon O. Lundberg, M.D., Ph.D.; Mauro Maniscalo, M.D.; Matteo Sofia, M.D., Ph.D.; Lars Lundblad, M.D., Ph.D.; and Eddie Weitzberg, M.D., Ph.D., "Humming, Nitric Oxide, and Paranasal Sinus Obstruction," *JAMA* 289, no. 3 (2003): 302–3.

JOHN BEAULIEU, N.D., PH.D., is one of the foremost philosophers and major innovators in the area of sound healing therapies. A world-renowned speaker, composer, pianist, and naturopathic doctor, Dr. Beaulieu has pioneered a technique called BioSonic Repatterning, a natural method of healing and consciousness development using tuning forks and other sound modalities based on the sonic ratios inherent in nature. He is author of *Music and Sound in the Healing Arts* and *Human Tuning: Sound Healing with Tuning Forks*. He lectures and performs worldwide and conducts training seminars for practitioners in the healing arts. His website is: **www.biosonics.com**.

Acknowledgments

We'd like to take this opportunity to offer our heartfelt thanks and appreciation to the many people who have contributed their time, energy, and support in helping to bring our book into manifestation.

We are grateful to the many people at Inner Traditions who have assisted our work, with special accolades to managing editor, Jeanie Levitan, assistant to the managing editor, Patricia Rydle, and our copy editor, Nancy Ringer. And we offer our greatest thanks to our project editor, Laura Schlivek. We are most grateful to acquisitions editor Jon Graham, who has been a longtime supporter of our work with sound healing. We also offer much thanks to Erica Robinson, who gave us her time so generously.

We are exceptionally grateful and honored to extend our appreciation to Dr. John Beaulieu for writing the foreword for our book and for his initiations into the sound current through humming. We wish to thank John and his wife, Thea, longtime colleagues and friends, for all their wonderful support.

We'd like to honor and thank some of the many people who truly helped initiate the concept of this book through their use of humming as a vehicle for healing and transformation. These include Jim Albani, for his story of humming at the Mall of America; Sarah "Saruah" Benson, for her activations of sonic compassion through humming;

Vickie Dodd, for her exceptional knowledge and teachings on how humming can be used to heal; Dr. Charles Eagle, for his guidance in finding the scientific research and data; Don Campbell, for his awareness of the subject; Ed and Deb Shapiro, for sharing their knowledge of bhramari pranayama; and Sri Swami Satchidananda, for his spiritual essence.

We know that it "takes a village" to bring a book full cycle, and our book is no exception. We therefore wish to thank our family and many friends who have been with us suffering the birth pangs of this creation. We especially thank Gregg Braden, Dr. Steve Brown, Dr. Ann Marie Chiasson, Tony Davis, Trevor Earth, Dr. Bea Knight-Johnson, Dr. George Lindenfeld, Dr. Bruce and Margaret Lipton, Mary Magdalena, Dr. Peter Guy Manners, John Stuart Reid, Makasha and Katharine Roske, Alec Sims, Dr. Valerie Solheim, Lama Tashi, Joan Vann, Dr. Phil Weber, Jim Wright, and Patricia Kay Youngson.

We give thanks to our families, whose love for us has truly assisted in maintaining the energy to create this book: our son, Joshua Goldman; our parents, Andrew and Bettye Pullman and Rose and Irving Goldman; our brothers and sisters, Richard and Peter Goldman, Rick Pullman, and Suzanne Strauss; and to all our nieces and nephews.

Finally, with loving kindness, we acknowledge and dedicate this book to you, dear reader. May these words assist in manifesting beneficial shifts and changes in you and all whom you may touch. We send blessings of light and love through sound to all who pass through these pages!

Introduction

Welcome to *The Humming Effect*. No doubt it took some feat of consciousness for you to pick up a book about humming. To our knowledge, this is the first book devoted to this subject—and that is why we have written it. Humming may be one of the most powerful natural abilities that we possess, yet most of us are completely unaware of it. We hope to reverse that situation.

This book is about conscious humming—that is, humming with a specific purpose or expectation, rather than simply humming without awareness. As you'll find out in the pages of this book, when you bring your conscious attention to the practice of humming, it becomes an extraordinary vehicle for healing and transformation. Humming is easy, and it has marvelous beneficial effects, from lowering blood pressure and heart rate to stimulating the release of vital hormones such as melatonin and nitric oxide. These positive results have been scientifically validated, and they promote not just physical health but happiness and a general sense of well-being.

We have been using sound as a therapeutic and transformational tool for a very long time—between us, we've put in over half a century of research, experience, and teaching the power of sound for healing. Jonathan is a leading pioneer in the field of sound healing and an expert in the field of harmonics. He is also an award-winning composer of music for healing and meditation. Andi is a holistic psychotherapist specializing in sound therapy and has worked with Jonathan in the field of sound healing for the past twenty years. While researching and writing this book, even with all these years of experience, we have uncovered surprising information on the simple act of humming. We trust that the power of humming will also surprise you.

The initial idea for writing a book on humming was to help initiate mainstream audiences into the healing power of their own self-created sound. In our experience, when people hear the words *sound healing,* their eyes tend to glaze over. They do not know what it is, they think it sounds esoteric, and they are uninterested in learning more. Many people immediately assume that they would have to have some musical ability, whether playing an instrument or singing, to practice sound healing. But humming requires no special skills—anyone can hum, and anyone can experience the extraordinary benefits that can result from their own self-created sound. This is not to say that humming cannot be musical, but it is not necessary. Humming is simply sound—vibrations that we all can use for healing and transformation.

The Humming Effect is designed primarily to educate readers about the innate power of humming and to give them experiences with their own self-created sound. Even if you have been working in the field of sound healing for as many years as we have, you may have been focused on vowel sounds or mantras or tuning forks or crystal bowls or unique instruments that generate special frequencies for healing. But odds are that the lowly hum has largely escaped your attention. We can guarantee that the information and exercises in this book will allow you to experience the world of humming in ways that you might never before have imagined.

The first part of this book, "Basic Principles," focuses on sound in general and the components of self-created sounds that are necessary to integrate conscious humming into your life. We'll deal specifically with the physics of sound as energy and how and why it has the ability to heal. As you learn the basic principles of sound healing, you will come to understand why, indeed, sound may be the fundamental creational energy of the universe.

We begin by exploring the innate power of your own voice and then introduce you to the physiological benefits of self-created sounds—data culled from various peer-reviewed, scientifically validated research studies. No doubt you will find this material quite fascinating. It is *so* fascinating, in fact, that you may be a bit skeptical about it. But we assure you, it is all accurate and all astonishing.

We then go on to address the importance and power of our breath while we are humming. It is indeed necessary to learn how to breathe in a proper manner—slowly and deeply—in order to truly experience the magnificent energy of sound. Without breath, there can be no sound. After we have explored breath, we will begin guiding you through some fundamental exercises that will allow you to experience how self-created sound can affect different parts of your body. For many, this awareness alone will be life changing.

We continue our journey of sound by delving into the extraordinary manner in which intention, or consciousness, has the ability to affect not only the sounds we create but our entire reality. Our intention enhances and amplifies the effects of our self-created sounds.

Part 2 of this book, "Practice Makes Perfect," focuses on guiding you, the reader, through exercises that will allow you to experience different humming techniques. We will start at a rudimentary level and progress to advanced forms of humming practices. Along the way, you will discover how to experience humming in different parts of your body. You will also begin to learn how to encode different levels of consciousness—belief, intent, visualization, and more—into your humming practice.

We will next explore methods of humming that are considered to be highly advanced practices in the yogic tradition. You will discover, as did we, the power that can manifest from these practices. And please know that it is not necessary to hold any sort of spiritual or religious beliefs when experimenting with these exercises; they simply are powerful tools for transformation, manifesting via the realm of humming.

We will culminate our journey in chapter 8, "The Humming Hypothesis," in which we share some of the groundbreaking work being done in the fields of sound, vibration, and the brain. And while we cannot prove with certainty the theories and connections that we speculate on, you will no doubt find the ideas and research we share with you to be both intriguing and astounding. It may well prove to be among the most important and groundbreaking material you will have come across.

Throughout the book you will see notes instructing you to listen to one or more of the audio tracks that accompany the text. We have provided recordings of vocal examples for some of the exercises in this book because sometimes hearing someone else practicing the sound of an exercise can help you follow along. However, everyone makes sound differently, and we do not want you to try to duplicate the sounds that we have recorded. These recordings are simply to give you an idea of the type of sound we would like you to create. Please make your own sound that resonates with you. See the section titled "How to Use *The Humming Effect* Instructional Audio Tracks" at the end of this book for assistance on using the audio tracks.

We ask that, first and foremost, you enjoy yourself. There is no competition with regard to how well or badly you create the sounds called for in this book; there is no contest to see if you can make them louder or longer than anyone else. These sounds are simply tools that allow you to experience inner resonance.

We are truly excited to be taking this journey into the world of humming with you. Babies can hum. The elderly can hum. Everyone can hum! And the results are truly a positive and powerful transformation. We have undergone our own metamorphosis through the power of the hum, and now, as advocates for sound healing, we hope that *The Humming Effect* can serve to guide you through your own powerful healing experience.

We thank you for having picked up this book—and for having stayed with us this far. You have already taken the first step on a journey that will allow you to explore realms of consciousness and vibration that will both entice and delight you. Enjoy!

PART I

Basic Principles

1
Why Hum?
The Power of Our Voice

This is a book about humming—one of the simplest and yet most profound sounds we can make. We can all hum. The very young can hum. The very old can hum. If you have a voice, you can hum. And that hum has extraordinary abilities that can be utilized for healing and much more.

Like humming, the intention of this book is simple and, yes, profound: to introduce you to sound and the power of your own voice. At a most basic level, sound is nothing more than vibration. But vibration has a powerful energy. The vibration of an opera singer's voice can break glass. The vibration of the humble hum can affect subatomic particles and shift molecular structures. We are not talking about music now—which many categorize into different genres, such as classical, rock, jazz, and so on. We are simply referring to sound, which is classified as vibration. These vibrations have the ability to heal and transform.

As noted, one of the simplest sounds we can create is the hum. Humming has extraordinary physiological effects, reducing stress, inducing calm, enhancing sleep, and healing us in incredible ways. In addition, as we discovered in our research on humming, the more specific our focus upon the hum, the more advanced its benefit.

In this book, we will move from the more basic aspects of this seemingly simple sound to a deeper understanding that some of the oldest spiritual texts in the world suggest that the "Word" we find in the Beginning (or as written in the Old Testament: "And the Lord said: 'Let there be Light!'") was in actuality the humming of energy. The ancient mystic masters understood that everything is vibration.

The subtitle of this book, "Sound Healing for Health and Happiness," makes a grand promise. As we have delved deeper and deeper into the subject, we have seen, time and again, the evidence: humming can improve not only your health but also the quality of your life, contributing greatly to your happiness.

Let us now take a look at some of the proven effects of humming—positive benefits that have been documented in well-established peer-reviewed journals. We were quite surprised to find that any research at all had been done on the benefits of humming. We'd like to share this research with you because the results are quite stunning.

Reduced Blood Pressure and Heart Rate

We would like to begin by acknowledging our first source. From Nepal Medical College we find a study with a most interesting name and most important data. The article is called "Immediate Effect of a Slow Pace Breathing Exercise Bhramari Pranayama on Blood Pressure and Heart Rate."* If you were wondering, bhramari pranayama is an advanced yogic exercise from the Hindu tradition, which we will discuss in chapter 7. It is basically humming combined with deep breathing. That's all. Yet from this medical school in a small (but highly enlightened) country comes proof positive of the ability of humming to lower blood pressure and heart rate.

As the authors note, participants in the study practiced bhramari pranayama by humming for five minutes at a time, focusing on creating "a humming nasal sound mimicking the sound of a humming wasp." Five minutes seems to be the minimum time necessary for sound to

---

*T. Pramanik, B. Pudasaini, and R. Prajapati, *Nepal Medical College Journal* 12, no. 3 (September 2010): 154–57.

create an effect on our body. The slow-paced humming caused both the systolic and diastolic blood pressure of participants to decrease significantly, accompanied by a slight decrease in heart rate. Thus, as the authors conclude, this type of humming induced "parasympathetic dominance" on the cardiovascular system.

For those of you missing your Ph.D. in anatomy, the autonomic nervous system has two different branches. The sympathetic nervous system is the one that causes what is known as the "fight or flight" response, which basically puts us in a state of stress. The parasympathetic nervous system can be thought of as the "stress eraser"—it puts us back in a state of balance. Interestingly, the primary parasympathetic nerve is the vagus nerve. This nerve is highly associated with our sense of perceiving (listening) and creating sound (vocalization). It is responsible for carrying the nerve impulses that slow heart rate, dilate blood vessels, activate digestion, and store energy. Our voice, our breathing, our heart rate, and our digestion are all affected by this nerve, which is, in turn, affected by sound.

We ask that you stop for a moment and think about the importance of this therapeutic aspect of humming. The bottom line is that humming can reduce your heart rate and lower your blood pressure. Essentially, it can reduce your stress response. And that includes reducing all those nasty hormones associated with stress, such as cortisol. Hmmmmm . . .

The limbic system is the part of the brain that includes the amygdala, hippocampus, thalamus, hypothalamus, basal ganglia, and cingulate gyrus. The amygdala is the portion of the brain that controls emotion. The limbic system regulates autonomic and endocrine functions, particularly in response to emotional stimuli. When the limbic system is activated, we often experience the "fight or flight" phenomenon and experience stress.

More research on the use of sound to lower stress came from the National Institute of Mental Health and Neuroscience in India. A 2011 study titled "Neurohemodynamic correlates of 'Om' chanting: A pilot functional magnetic resonance imaging study" from the International Journal of Yoga showed similar aspects of the stress-reducing power of the hum.* With this study, using functional Magnetic Resonance Imaging (fMRI), it was found that there was deactivation of the limbic system when participants of this study chanted *Om*. As noted, the limbic system encompasses various parts of the brain that deal with emotion. Deactivation of the limbic system provides significant reduction of stress and enhanced calmness for the individual.

The *Om* sound is considered very similar to humming and is often considered to be essentially the same sound. For this study, the *Om* chanting was compared with pronunciation of the sound *ssss*. When this *ssss* was sounded, there was no limbic deactivation. When the *Om* was chanted, limbic deactivation occurred. This indicates that, as opposed to many other sounds, there may be something quite special about the ability of humming to reduce stress.

If there is a number-one killer on this planet, it's stress. This fact should not be a great revelation to anyone who has paid even the least bit of attention to the media's coverage of health topics over the last thirty years. Stress causes heart attacks. Stress causes strokes. Stress causes cancer. Stress causes neuron depletion, which damages your brain. Shall we continue?

The studies from the Nepal Medical College and the National Institute of Mental Health and Neuroscience in India both demonstrated that just five minutes of humming can radically reduce stress. It's that powerful and that simple. So, before you reach for that Xanax, that glass of wine, or whatever you use to unwind, perhaps you'll take five minutes for a finely tuned sonically prescribed hum.

Increased Nitric Oxide Levels

Nitric oxide is a very important molecule. It is, in fact, so important that it was named "Molecule of the Year" by the prestigious journal

---

*B G. Kalyani, G. Venkatasubramanian, R. Arasappa, N. P. Rao, S. V. Kalmady, R. V. Behere, H. Rao, et al., *International Journal of Yoga* 4, no. 1 (2011): 3–6.

Science back in 1992. Among its attributes, it enhances our immune system, our cardiovascular system, and our respiratory system. In particular, nitric oxide causes vasodilation, or widening of our blood vessels, which increases blood flow and decreases blood pressure.

The relationship between sound and nitric oxide was initially observed at the Neuroscience Research Institute of the State University of New York, when research subjects simply listened to soothing music and experienced greater levels of nitric oxide. This relaxation response was also observed in the application of specially designed tuning fork frequencies, which enhanced self-resonating sounds such as humming.

Researchers in Sweden studying the effects of humming found that it triggered the release of nitric oxide in a localized area of the body—the nasal cavity.* This is not surprising, since, as we will discuss later in the book, in order to hum properly, your nasal cavity has to be vibrating. But we'd also like to take into account the fact that it's relatively easy to measure the release of nitric oxide in your nasal cavity. All you need is an inexpensive medical instrument to measure this. You would insert it in a person's nose, have him or her hum, and measure the amount of nitric oxide that is released. The release of nitric oxide and the way it affects us may be localized to a specific organ (depending on the metabolic needs of a particular tissue, as during strenuous exercise), or it may be systemic.

Nearly two-thirds of the peer-reviewed papers we found on Medline (a reputable online database of biomedical research), that explored some therapeutic aspect of humming, focused on this phenomenon of nitric oxide being released in the nasal cavity. We were quite pleased by all this documented research on humming. Since the release of nitric oxide opens up the sinuses, the next time you have a stuffy nose, just hum for a few minutes and it'll open up your nasal cavity.

---

*Eddie Weitzberg and Jon O. N. Lundberg, "Humming Greatly Increases Nasal Nitric Oxide," *American Journal of Respiratory and Critical Care Medicine* 166, no. 2 (2002): 144–45.

But we think there is more to the effects of the release of nitric oxide—much more. Our colleague, renowned sound researcher Dr. John Beaulieu, was invited to participate in an experiment involving nitric oxide. As part of the experiment, he examined whether the sound of a tuning fork affected cells in a petri dish and caused them to release nitric oxide. It did. When they first registered the cells' release of nitric oxide, Dr. Beaulieu's scientific partners thought it was an error. They had him repeat his part in this experiment again and again, and each time, the cells consistently released nitric oxide.*

In other words, even cells isolated in a petri dish will release nitric oxide when stimulated by sound vibration. While further research has yet to be done, we'd like to present our first hypothesis: when you are humming, and particularly when you are projecting your hum to specific parts of your body, you are actually causing cells in those parts of your body to release nitric oxide—with all the associated health benefits.

From our perspective, as well as many others, humming can act as an internal sonic massage. As Don Campbell, sonic expert and author of *The Mozart Effect*, states: "Humming actually massages the body from the inside out."† This concept of massaging the body through self-created sounds is a principle of vibrational healing that most sound therapists as well as massage therapists find to be true.

As we've noted, the initial research had to do with the release of nitric oxide in the nasal cavity. It makes sense that researchers looked here first, because humming requires the nasal cavity—if you hold your nose, you simply can't hum. But as you'll soon discover, it is not only possible but relatively easy—particularly with the use of

---

*John Beaulieu, "Otto 128 Tuning Fork and Nitric Oxide Response," Cell Dynamics Lab, unpublished raw data set.
†Don G. Campbell, "Chanting, Listening and the Electronic Ear: The Pioneering Work of Dr. Alfred Tomatis," Sound Healer's Association website, available at http://www .soundhealersassociation.org/don-campbell-chanting-listening-and-the-electronic-ear (accessed February 27, 2017).

intent and a slight variation of pitch—to project a humming sound to different parts of your body and cause those parts of your body to vibrate.

The nasal cavity, other parts of the skull, and the chest are easy areas of the body to resonate with humming. You'll experience this once we begin our humming exercises. Given that the brain and heart—vital organs—are located in the head and chest, we'd like to suggest that vibrating these areas of the body can be extremely helpful for our overall health, possibly even going so far as to prevent or mitigate stroke and heart disease.

Research has shown sound—vibration—stimulates cells to release nitric oxide. Is it possible that humming, then, could be used to resonate different areas of the body, causing the release of nitric oxide and opening up blood flow in those areas? Could we use humming to target, for example, neurological health, heart health, circulatory health, and so on? Hmmmmm . . .

Increased Lymphatic Circulation

The lymphatic system is responsible for the circulation and filtering of lymph, the fluid that drains from tissues into the blood. It also acts as a highway, transporting white blood cells to and from the lymph nodes into the bones, as well as carrying antigen-presenting cells to the lymph nodes, enhancing our immune response. You get rid of a lot of bodily toxins through the lymphatic system—toxins that can be quite damaging to your health.

One of the effects of humming (and self-created sound in general) is increased oxygen levels in the cells. This is partly due to the fact that when you hum, you breathe deeply, which helps oxygenate your cells. But certainly the release of nitric oxide is also a contributing factor. This also applies to the lymphatic system, which is a subset of the circulatory system.

There are sonic machines that use sound for the purpose of encouraging lymphatic drainage when the lymphatic system is blocked.* Since, as previously suggested, we are able to massage ourselves internally with self-created sound, vibrating our organs and glands, sounds such as humming could be used for the same purpose as these sonic machines. When you hum, whether generally or directed to a specific area of your body, you are also vibrating, massaging, and activating other areas of your body as well—including your cells, your circulatory system, and your lymphatic circulation. Nitric oxide is also released. As you increase lymphatic circulation, you increase the amount of oxygen in your cells. All of this is able to improve your immune system and more. Hmmmmm . . .

Increased Melatonin Levels

Melatonin is a hormone that is associated with the circadian rhythms of several biological functions. Most of us have heard of melatonin and usually think of it as having something to do with sleep. In fact, some people with sleeping problems take melatonin to help them sleep. In humans, melatonin is produced by the pineal gland, located in the center of the brain. Besides its function as synchronizer of the biological clock, melatonin is a powerful free-radical scavenger and wide-spectrum antioxidant.

Research indicates that melatonin supports our immune system and has anti-inflammatory effects. Some studies suggest that melatonin might be useful in fighting infectious disease. Other studies have shown that melatonin plays a crucial part in the aging process and that it may act as an antiaging agent. Research into melatonin for treatment of depression continues, as do studies on the effects of melatonin on cancer as well as the use of melatonin for addressing learning disabilities, memory disorders, and Alzheimer's disease. Though much of the research to

---

*Ramona Moody French, *The Complete Guide to Lymph Drainage Massage,* 2nd. ed. (Clifton Park, N.Y.: Milady, 2011).

date has been inconclusive, many ongoing studies show great promise.

Our Canadian colleague Dr. Ranjie Singh was the first to demonstrate that self-created sounds stimulate the pineal gland to release melatonin, and he describes his research in his groundbreaking book, *Self-Healing: Powerful Techniques.* The pineal gland regulates many different bodily functions, including sleep patterns. In many esoteric traditions, it was thought of as the "seat of the soul" or the "third eye." This pinecone shaped endocrine gland is quite small but also quite important. Initially, Dr. Singh conducted his experiments on the pineal gland in a rather simple way—he divided his test subjects into two groups, had one group practice what he calls "meditative intonation," and then tested his subjects' urine for melatonin levels. He found significantly higher melatonin levels in the group that had practiced intonation. Dr. Singh's ongoing work with humming and melatonin has since been published in many prestigious journals.[*]

Melatonin supplements are readily available; you can buy them at most grocery stores. However, they're not nearly as effective as the melatonin that your own body produces.

The fact that you can stimulate the pineal gland to release melatonin through humming is extraordinary. You can potentially enhance your sleep, your immune system, your aging process, and a whole lot more through your own self-created sound. Hmmmmm . . .

Endorphin Release

Endorphins are powerful opiate-like neurotransmitters that block pain and contribute to feelings of pleasure and euphoria. Sometimes people talk about an "endorphin rush," a sensation that is almost narcotic-like in its ability to make us feel good.

---

[*]See, for example, the following article about a study that incorporates Dr. Singh's meditative intonation: N. Absolon, T. Truant, L. Balneaves, et al., "'I Can't Sleep': Gathering the evidence for an innovative intervention for insomnia in cancer patients," *Canadian Oncology Nursing Journal* 24, no. 3 (2014): 154–59.

The pituitary gland and the hypothalamus produce en
just during times of pain and stress but also when we are ac
or enjoying ourselves. Exercise, sex, and just about any activity
us feel good, including playing music, dancing, and singing, ca
endorphin release. These natural opiates are also generated when we hum.*

Think about the times when you tend to find yourself humming.
Odds are, you hum when you're happy—that is, happiness leads to
humming. Could the opposite also be true? Could humming lead to
happiness?

If you've spent any time around very young children, you'll have
noticed that they seem to like to hum—at least when they're content.
They certainly cry when they're irritable. Perhaps humming is not only
a way to express that we're feeling good, perhaps it's also a way of inducing those good feelings. Like nursing and laughing, humming may be
one of the first natural impulses that makes us feel good. Maybe it's the
endorphins? Maybe it's not. We can't ask the babies, but we can speculate that it may in fact be the endorphins and perhaps a lot more.

Jonathan has a story that involves humming and most probably
endorphins. It was one of the first times he'd become aware of the
importance of humming. He was sitting outside on the veranda of a
friend's home with John Lilly, MD. Dr. Lilly was a neuroscientist and
writer who explored human consciousness, dolphin communication,
and the borders of reality. Trained in medicine, psychoanalysis, and bio-
physics, John carved out an eclectic career that shifted between research
published in scientific journals and self-experimentation codified
mainly in books aimed at fellow students of spirituality and expanded
consciousness. His life inspired two movies: *Day of the Dolphin* and
Altered States. Dr. Lilly passed away in 2001, but at the time Jonathan
met him, he was quite a celebrity.

Dr. Lilly and Jonathan were both guests at a party in their honor

*L. J. Seltzer, T. E. Ziegler, and S. D. Pollak, "Social Vocalizations Can Release Oxytocin
in Humans," *Proceedings of the Royal Society B: Biological Sciences* 277, no 1694 (2010):
2661–66.

while they were in Los Angeles teaching and lecturing. There were upwards of a hundred people at this gathering. Jonathan went outside to escape the crowd, and there he found John Lilly. The two of them sat there by themselves. Neither spoke. As they sat, Jonathan realized that Dr. Lilly was continuously humming. He would breathe in and then, as he exhaled, very softly and slowly he would hum—an audible vibration.

It occurred to Jonathan that Dr. Lilly was perhaps humming as a self-soothing mechanism to balance and align his nervous system. Since he was a well-known proponent of altered states of consciousness, it was also possible that he had discovered a method of using the hum to create a waveform that he could travel on with his consciousness. Perhaps it was a combination of both.

Finally, Jonathan asked Dr. Lilly, "John, are you doing that consciously?"

Dr. Lilly continued his humming for a moment and then replied, "I no longer know what consciousness is." He went on to explain that he thought of his mind as a mansion with many rooms. Each of the rooms represented a different aspect of reality, and each of these realities was based upon a different aspect of consciousness. It was an extraordinary answer to what Jonathan had thought was a simple question. After Dr. Lilly's reply, Jonathan simply said, "Thank you" and went back inside to join the party.

We share this story with you because it seems quite possible that Dr. Lilly was receiving some remarkable benefit from humming. Perhaps he was simply enjoying the experience of the endorphins being released. Perhaps it was something more. As you will discover later on, it is quite possible to use humming to shift and positively change our emotional and psychological states.

While we are on the topic of endorphins, it's important to acknowledge that humming has the ability to reduce pain. While we ourselves have experienced it, we do not have the data to validate it. This effect could be entirely attributable to the release of endorphins. There may, however, be other causes that contribute to this effect. Years ago, the *New York Times* wrote an article on the healing effects of self-created sound and interviewed Jonathan on this subject. Upon being asked why such sounds seemed to help reduce pain, his first answer was, "Endorphins!" But then he suggested that there might be other factors—everything from the idea that humming created a distraction that caused our brain to (momentarily at least) forget about the pain to the speculation that perhaps when we made self-created sound we were somehow able to create a vibration at the site of the pain, thus causing a kind of sonic massage that helped reduce the pain.

Recently, we reviewed research that showed that participants who made sound while plunging their hand into freezing cold water were able to withstand longer durations of time in the water than those who had to silently plunge their hand into the water. Regrettably, this research did not offer an explanation as to why this phenomenon occurred. It simply noted the result.

So . . . Endorphins? Distraction? Sonic massage? Or something else? Regardless, the fact that you can use humming to make yourself feel better and reduce physical pain is an extraordinary benefit. We'll go into techniques for pain reduction using the hum later in this book.

Oxytocin Release

Oxytocin is a hormone produced by the hypothalamus and stored and secreted by the pituitary gland. Oxytocin is associated with situations involving close relationships, such as the deep sharing in friendships, intimacy in making love, nursing a baby, and so on. That's why it's known as the "trust hormone" or "love hormone." It seems to facilitate a bonding—an empathic sort of feeling between people.

Activities that allow us to make sounds with others, like singing, making music, or even humming together, can stimulate the release of oxytocin.* This may help explain why our hearts and souls feel so

---

*Seltzer, Ziegler, and Pollak, "Social Vocalizations Can Release Oxytocin in Humans."

nourished when we sing with a group, such as a church or community choir. In fact, even making a simple sound with another person, such as an elongated *Om* or *ah* sound (known as "toning"), will help elevate the level of trust between you.

From our perspective, whether it's the release of oxytocin, endorphins, melatonin, or whatnot, numerous biochemical factors are stimulated simultaneously in our bodies when we utilize self-created sounds in some capacity. There's no doubt that the release of these hormones contributes to the overall positive effects we might experience when we hum. Hmmmmm . . .

To summarize, when we make self-created sounds, a number of beneficial therapeutic effects occur, including:

- Increased oxygen in cells
- Lowered blood pressure and heart rate
- Increased lymphatic circulation
- Increased levels of melatonin
- Reduced levels of stress-related hormones
- Release of endorphins
- Increased levels of nitric oxide
- Release of oxytocin

In this chapter, we have focused on some of the proven physiological benefits of humming, such as reduction of stress, increased relaxation, enhanced sleep, and healthier hearts, minds, and spirits. We trust that this exploration has been more than enough to answer this chapter's headline question, "Why hum?"

Now let's move on and delve into the physics of sound. This investigation will help explain how and why sound has such potential to heal.

2

The Physics of Sound

How and Why Sound Heals

An examination of the majority of spiritual paths and religions on this planet reveals an overriding belief that sound was the primary force of creation. Examples of this come from the Old Testament ("And God said, 'Let there be Light'") and the New Testament ("In the beginning was the Word"). It comes from many other traditions—Egyptian, Hopi, Mayan, Polynesian, and more—which all have creation myths that invoke the power of sound. It is said in the Hindu spiritual path that "Nada Brahman"—everything is sound. Even from a Western scientific perspective, we talk about the "Big Bang," signifying that the creation of the universe was somehow sonic in origin.

Modern scientists, like our ancient mystics, tell us that everything is in a state of vibration, from the electrons moving around the nucleus of an atom to planets in distant galaxies spinning around their suns. From the very tiny to the very large, everything vibrates. As many of our modern physicists understand, energy and matter are interrelated. Thus, if all forms of energy are putting out a vibration, all that energy can be considered sound, whether we can hear it or not.

Frequency

Sound is energy that travels as a wave. The wave enters our ears and travels through our auditory pathways into our brain, ultimately affecting our breathing, heart rate, and nervous system. We experience this wavelike energy primarily as a phenomenon that we hear. However, these waves also pass into our body, affecting us on a cellular level.

Sounds are measured in cycles per second, or frequency, as measured in hertz (Hz). Slow-moving waves of sound create deep tones. A sound with a frequency of 60 Hz, for example, is very bassy and low. A sound with fast waves, such as 1,000 cycles per second, would be a relatively trebly and high-pitched. The lowest note on a piano has a frequency of about 24 Hz, and the highest note is around 5,000 Hz.

Our range of hearing extends from around 16 Hz to around 16,000 Hz (or sometimes higher—young children, for example, can hear upwards of 18,000 Hz or more). However, just because we can't hear something doesn't mean a sound isn't being created. As an example, our friends in the ocean, the dolphins, can project and receive frequencies upwards of 180,000 Hz—that's more than ten times our best range of hearing.

Sounds with a frequency below the human level of hearing are called infrasound; sounds with a frequency above the human level of hearing are called ultrasound.

Resonance

Knowing that all matter vibrates, we can move on to explore the idea that every object—including every organ, bone, and tissue in our body—has *resonance*, or a natural vibratory state. There's been much speculation on how to determine the natural frequencies of a healthy organ. Some find that they are within the audible sonic range (between 16 Hz and 16,000 Hz). Others find that they fall well below this audible range or, like ultrasound, far above it. When the body is healthy and balanced, these vibrations are in harmony with each other. When the body is imbalanced, it is in a state of dissonance—the resonant qualities of its constituent parts are in disharmony.

One of the most extraordinary demonstrations of the effects of sound and resonance was conducted by a visionary Swiss doctor named Hans Jenny. Dr. Jenny's seminal work titled *Cymatics* (a Greek word that means "wave form"), whose first volume was published in 1967, showed the effects that sound waves have upon different types of material, including water, pastes, and other liquids. Dr. Jenny placed these substances on a steel plate and vibrated the plate with a crystal oscillator, which produced an exact frequency, and then he photographed the effects. He photographed liquid plastic (a material similar to Silly Putty) that formed into an object resembling a sea anemone, and lycopodium dust (a material similar to talcum powder) that took on shapes resembling the cells of the body. Some of his most amazing photos were of water, which took on astonishing geometric forms, depending upon the vibrational frequency that was used.

Dr. Jenny's work demonstrates the extraordinary power of vibration—that is, sound—to create form. While the structures and forms he created with sound were not living creatures, many of them certainly look as though they were. You can almost imagine that, with a "divine" sound coming from a sacred source, in the beginning the Word could indeed create life.

What is equally important with regard to Dr. Jenny's experiments is that the effects are repeatable. If you take the same substance and expose it to the same frequency that Dr. Jenny used, you will get the same result. This consistent structuring—a certain vibration leads to a certain form—is a manifestation of resonance. If the vibration changes, the structure changes in concert with it.

Several people have carried on Dr. Jenny's work in the twenty-first century, including Alexander Lauterwasser of Germany and John Stuart Reid of England. The following are two photos taken by Reid showing the beautiful geometric forms that water took on when vibrated by two diverse frequencies on a CymaScope, a device similar to Dr. Jenny's. When you think about the fact that the human body is mostly made of water, it's easy to realize how powerful the effects of sound can be upon us.

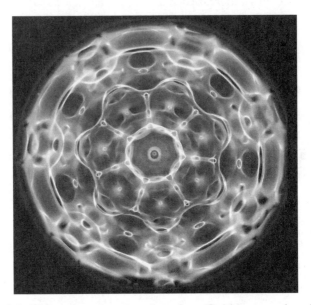

Fig. 2.1. The voice of author Jonathan Goldman rendered as a visual pattern by a CymaScope.

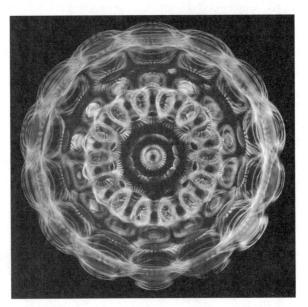

Fig. 2.2. A female voice mandala made visible by a CymaScope

Let's now examine two different (almost diametrically opposed) ways in which sound can be used for healing. Both involve the concept of resonance.

How Sound Can Heal: Method One

For this first method of healing with sound, let's visualize a healthy body like an orchestra that is playing all together in balance and harmony. Let's call this music the "symphony of the self."

Using this metaphor of the body as an orchestra, what happens when the second violin player loses his sheet music? Pretty soon that violin player might begin to play the wrong notes and the wrong rhythm. Usually, in a very short amount of time, the rest of the string section begins to sound off. In fact, as this dissonance develops, you'll begin to notice that there's something wrong with the entire orchestra. It just doesn't sound right.

This is akin to a part of our body vibrating out of its healthy resonance—it's vibrating out of tune and out of ease, and we then say that this part of our body is diseased (dis-eased). One of the basic principles of using sound as a healing modality is to restore the part of the body that is diseased back into a state of healthy resonance. It is very much like getting the sheet music back to that string player.

It seems appropriate at this time to honor Dr. Peter Guy Manners, one of Jonathan's mentors and one of the great pioneers in the field of sound therapy. Dr. Manners passed away at the turn of this century, but he had been engaged in the research and practice of sound healing since the 1950s. His work focused on finding the correct frequencies to restore healthy resonance to different parts of the body for different conditions. He created the "Cymatic Instrument" (now known by other names), which had the ability to project over six hundred different combinations of frequencies (which he called "commutations") in order to strengthen an imbalanced portion of our anatomy. Due to some legal issues, his work (and his instrument) was not as well known at the time as it perhaps could have been. However, today trained practitioners in the field of sound healing readily employ numerous devices based upon the work of Dr. Manners, with remarkable healing benefit.

Although we have been introduced to many different types of instruments designed for sound healing, our preferred instrument is one that doesn't require electricity or batteries, has an owner's manual that's really simple to use, and is free. This instrument is, of course, our own voice. And it's what we've been teaching for dozens of years.

Please note: we are not talking about using the voice in a musical fashion such as singing—that's entertainment. We're not talking about getting up in front of an audience and singing "Strangers in the Night" or whatever song turns you on. Here, in relation to sound specifically utilized for healing, we're talking about the concept of entrainment.

The term *entrainment* comes from physics, and it describes the way in which the vibrations of one object can affect the vibrations of another object. Through entrainment, we can synchronize or harmonize one vibration with another. For example, we can use our own voice to vocalize a tone through humming that can entrain vibrations in other parts of our bodies, bringing them into a state of balance.

There are many ways to use entrainment for sound healing. At a basic level, you can use vibration—humming—to restore the natural resonance of an organ or system. When an organ begins to vibrate out of its natural frequency, its energy becomes blocked. The organ then becomes vulnerable to potential imbalances—deterioration, disease, viruses, bacteria, and so on. When we reinforce its natural frequency, the organ's resonance is restored, it regains its energy, the intruder energy that was causing damage ceases to exist, and the organ is restored to health.

You might also use different rhythms to influence bodily pulses, such as our heartbeat, respiration, and brainwaves. Or you can use sounds that are slightly out of tune, called "beat frequencies," which can be applied in a specific manner to influence brain waves. We will discuss some of these uses of entrainment later in this book.

How Sound Can Heal: Method Two

With this second method, sound is used in an opposite manner. Instead of focusing on the organ and reinforcing its healthy, natural vibratory state, this method focuses on the intruder—that pathogen or energy that is causing harm to the organ.

You can find videos of people shattering wine glasses with their voices on YouTube. Even such reputable shows as the Discovery Channel's *MythBusters* have recorded the phenomenon. When a singer is able to match the resonance of the wine glass with his or her voice with great amplitude (volume), the glass begins to vibrate and ultimately shatters. This ability of sound to disintegrate matter has been known for a long time. Remember the story of Joshua and the walls of Jericho in the Old Testament? Joshua and his men blew horns and gave a great shout and the walls crumbled.

With sufficient amplitude, sound is powerful enough to cause any object to shatter when its resonant frequency matches that of the object. This second approach to sound healing focuses on using sound to disintegrate whatever pathogen, malignancy, or energy is causing harm to the body.

In the early 1930s, a scientist named Royal Rife invented an instrument that was said to be able to shatter cancer cells and their pathogenic precursors (he believed that all cancers were caused by bacteria and/or viruses) with high-frequency vibrations. He developed a microscope that allowed him to observe these pathogens, and then he worked with high-frequency vibrations to find the correct frequencies for destroying them. Whether his treatment of those with cancer still holds true or not, his work with high-frequency sound was incredible.

Recently, we were sent a link to a video for a TEDx Talk by Professor Anthony Holland, a musician-scientist at Skidmore College, discussing his work shattering cancer cells and bacteria with high-frequency vibrations. Among other things, the video has some astonishing visuals of this phenomenon occurring.* It truly demonstrates the power of sound to heal.

---

*To see the video, go to https://www.youtube.com/watch?v=1w0_kazbb_U.

Many of us are familiar with the use of high-frequency sound, called ultrasound, to construct images of babies in utero. These ultrasonic frequencies are also often used to disintegrate kidney stones. The possibilities don't stop there. For example, Jeff Elias, M.D., of the University of Virginia's medical school is using ultrasound to treat Parkinson-like tremors. We first heard of his work on the national nightly news. Dr. Elias was treating an elderly woman with such bad shaking from tremors that she could not write her name with any sort of legibility. Using an fMRI to view her brain, Dr. Elias trained a beam of highly focused sound energy on the area of the brain where damage had occurred. The procedure lasted less than a minute. About ten minutes later, the woman was asked to sign her name, and her script was lovely and legible.

Any surgery to address the woman's tremors would have been extensive, and recovery would have taken close to six months. In contrast, the ultrasound treatment was brief and noninvasive, and the woman's recovery time was almost instantaneous. It was astonishing. The reporter covering the story asked Dr. Elias what other conditions might be treated with sound. He suggested that there were many different possibilities. What is perhaps most significant about the work of Professor Holland and Dr. Elias is that it has been filmed, which vividly validates the power of sound to heal and transform.

Over the years that we have been working together with the power of sound, we have seen incredible things—tumors disappearing, broken bones healing, incurable chronic conditions immediately becoming better. We have also received many extraordinary testimonials from people who have utilized sound healing techniques with powerful results. But all these stories provide only anecdotal evidence. Without documentation, they can be hard to believe. This was why we began our book with scientific proof of the positive effects of humming, published in reputable journals and reviewed by qualified peers of the studies' authors. We look forward to the future when more data regarding the effects of these high-frequency sounds and new acceptance of these vibrations for healing will become available. We hope this book will help.

Amplitude

As previously noted, sound energy is defined as its amplitude. Amplitude is simply the loudness (or softness) of a sound, as measured in decibels. The human ear can be incredibly sensitive to sound. A normal conversation is about 70 decibels. A whisper is closer to 20 decibels.

The threshold of how much sound we are hearing today has been increasing astronomically. Once sounds above 70 decibels were rarely heard. Perhaps in a noisy factory we'd hear 90 or more decibels or when sitting in the front of an orchestral recital. One hundred years ago, the loudest sounds people normally heard were from a church organ on Sunday mornings, a thunderstorm, or if they were unfortunate enough, the cannons of war.

Today, however, it's commonplace to be blasted by the sound of a low flying jet plane creating waves of 110 decibels or more. Many rock 'n' roll bands have been found to create music that exceeds 130 decibels. It's become almost unusual to see someone walking down the street without a pair of earphones (or earbuds) feeding them music and, sadly, these sounds have the ability of playing back over 120 decibels at full volume.

The threshold of damage to our hearing from sound pressure is around 120 decibels. However, we do not experience pain in our ears until at least 140 decibels. This means we can be feeling comfortable about sound pressure levels, yet it can be doing damage to our hearing. For example, we can be listening to loud music of 120 decibels in a club without actually feeling pain and yet be doing damage to our hearing. We can begin to have hearing loss from listening to sounds at this volume. Many are concerned that we will soon have a generation of hearing impaired as a result.

Besides hearing impairment, loud sounds also trigger the "fight or flight" mechanism within us. This may be due to a time when we were more primitive. We'd hear the growl of a saber-toothed tiger and find ourselves high up in a tree before we were aware of what we'd heard.

Such reactions to loud sounds were lifesaving at one time in our evolution, but the reaction of our autonomic nervous system has not changed. Loud sounds, whether they are sirens from police cars, fire engines, or instruments playing music, still affect us in this way.

Once, we were visiting Venice Beach, California, having a wonderful time watching all the street performers. One man with an audience in front of him held up a one hundred dollar bill and told those listening that he would give this bill to any person who remained stationary after he had blindfolded them. He promised he would not touch them and that they would be perfectly safe. One testosterone-laden young man, who was obviously a body builder, came forth and volunteered. The street performer drew a chalk circle around this young man and then blindfolded him. We had a pretty good idea what would happen next. The performer took a balloon and brought it to the ear of the body builder. Then he pulled out a pin and popped the balloon. The young muscle man must have easily jumped a yard. Needless to say, he didn't get the one hundred dollars, but it was a great example of the power of loud sounds to affect us.

The only danger we've encountered with regard to the use of acoustic instruments or the voice is when the sound is so loud that it brings harm to someone, or has the potential of creating damage to our hearing. It's important to note that we have not encountered any potential damaging sounds through use of the voice, or other instruments when they aren't too loud. We suppose it's possible, but it's not something that's frequently found. But we wanted to bring the power of loud sounds to your attention as an important aspect of the physics of sound.

Ultrasound versus Audible Sound

Ultrasound treatment often utilizes extremely high frequencies, sometimes resonating at hundreds of thousands of cycles per second, and extremely high amplitude (volume). Perhaps because they are so far beyond our realm of hearing, they do not seem to damage our ears. However, sound can be used to target and destroy harmful cells, such as cancer, not just in the ultrasound range but in the audible range as well. Our colleague Fabien Maman, a French scientist, acupuncturist, and sound healer, conducted experiments in Paris more than twenty years ago utilizing this method of sound healing.

Working in a medical research lab, Maman utilized a xylophone to see how sound would affect cancer cells. He began with the note C and then went up the chromatic scale (C, C-sharp, D, D-sharp, E, F, F-sharp, G, G-sharp, A, A-sharp, B, and C—all the notes within an octave). He would strike a note, let it ring, wait for about a minute, and then hit the next higher note. According to Maman, the cancer cells, which were on a slide under a microscope, were more rigid than the healthy cells surrounding them. As the tones of the xylophone went higher and higher, the cancer cells began to be affected by the sounds, beginning to change shape, until around the notes A-sharp and B, when they would explode. Maman published some impressive photographs of his work in his book *The Tao of Sound*.

Both Maman and Dr. Holland (see pages 25, 26) used sound to target cancer cells. Maman used normal, audible sound; Dr. Holland used ultrasound. In both cases, the cancer cells were destroyed, while the healthy cells were unaffected. Despite the fact that one experiment utilized frequencies within the audible range (16 Hz to 16,000 Hz) and the other used frequencies in the many hundreds of thousands of Hz, the outcome of these procedures was very similar.

One reason why audible sound and ultrasound may be so much in resonance is due to a phenomenon of the physics of sound called "harmonics". Most people are unaware of harmonics, but they experience them every day since harmonics are an integral part of nearly every sound that we hear.

The study of harmonics is usually relegated to an advanced study of the physics of sound. Harmonics are also one of the most mysterious and complex aspects of sound. Jonathan's first book was dedicated to the subject, titled *Healing Sounds: The Power of Harmonics,* and it explored this subject in detail. The information in this portion of this book comes from *Healing Sounds.*

When we look at clear light such as sunlight, we are really looking at a composite of different colored light rays that create the light spectrum. However, they blend together to create the clear light of sunlight that we see. We can take a prism and hold it into sunlight and suddenly the colors of the rainbow appear. Through a prism, the colors of the light spectrum appear. Though all these various colors are present, they have merged together to create clear light and we need a prism or some other apparatus to be able to observe them.

Harmonics are an aspect of sound that interact in a similar manner and can be considered the colors of sound. Whenever a sound is created in nature, there are a multitudinous number of different frequencies that simultaneously occur and have merged together. The lowest frequency that is created is called the fundamental frequency. It is the most audible frequency we hear. All frequencies that are higher are called harmonics or overtones.

Harmonics are mathematic multiples of that first fundamental frequency. If we strike a string, for example and the fundamental frequency of that string is vibrating at 100 cycles per second (Hz) simultaneously, numerous other vibrations are occurring with that string—these vibrations are the harmonics or overtones of that string. The first harmonic is vibrating at twice the speed of the fundamental frequency—at 200 Hz. The second harmonic is vibrating three times as fast as that fundamental—300 Hz. The next harmonic is vibrating four times as fast (400 Hz), and the harmonic after is vibrating five times as fast at 500 Hz. These whole number multiples of the fundamental frequency keep going—potentially until infinity.

The frequency of 100 Hz, which we used in the above example of the vibrating string, was merely utilized to make the mathematics easier to understand. Any possible fundamental frequency can manifest the harmonic series. And as noted, it is not merely a vibrating string that produces harmonics, but all sound created by instruments, as well as our voice and all sounds in nature.

When we hear a sound such as a single note being played on an instrument, we are truly hearing a multitude of sounds that are simultaneously occurring. In an electronic laboratory, the harmonics were removed from three instruments using special filters. Upon listening to these instruments without their harmonics, it became impossible to tell them apart. Yet, under normal circumstance, it is not difficult to distinguish between a violin, a trumpet, and a piano.

All the different sounds we hear are the result of multitudinous harmonics blending together. This can be a real "ear opener" to those unaware of this phenomenon. Often, it leads to a level of deeper listening for people hearing sounds within sounds—the results of our beginning to perceive overtones. While all sounds that are created in nature are the results of the multiple vibrating frequencies that we call harmonics, it is specific harmonics that create the "timbre" or tone color of a sound. This is why, for example, a violin sounds like a violin, a piano sounds like a piano, and a tuba sounds like a tuba. The harmonics of these different instruments all slightly vary. The harmonics are the same, being mathematical multiples of the base or fundamental frequency. However, the strength of each harmonic that is created will be different depending upon what instrument is making the sound. The most prominent harmonics are called "formants" and they are responsible for the uniqueness of all sounds.

Another aspect of harmonics that we'd like to bring to your awareness is that the mathematics of harmonics can be observed throughout the universe. Harmonics correspond to an underlying framework existing in chemistry, physics, crystallography, astronomy, architecture, spectroanalysis, botany, and the study of other nature sciences. The relationship expressed in the periodic table of elements resembles the overtone structure in music, as do the orbital distances of the planets.

We've probably all experienced a car driving by with the speakers playing sounds so deep that some things in the house began to shake. This is an example of the sympathetic resonance of sound created by harmonics.

We can usually hear the first fifteen or so harmonics. But harmonics continue multiplying, faster and faster, creating sounds that transcend our realm of hearing. This is one reason why it is possible that a sound within the audible range can resonate in the ultrasonic bandwidth as well and vice versa. Through harmonics, audible sounds are able to sympathetically resonate and affect both the infrasound and ultrasound range.

Dr. Robert Becker of Cornell University experimented with using electric frequencies for healing, and he chronicled his research in his 1985 book, *The Body Electric.* He suggested that with electricity, the less violent and the more gentle the current, the more effective it would be. We often think that the same could hold true for sound. Often when people become aware of the power of sound, they become enamored with it and convinced that "more is better" and "louder is better." From our perspective, neither of these beliefs is valid or true. Maman's work with sound provides evidence for our belief in the healing power of sound in the audible, everyday range of human hearing.

Before we close this chapter, we'd like to bring your attention to an interesting sound bite that's been around for almost thirty years. It's from a 1988 *New York Times* article about the uses of ultrasound, which, in speaking of focused beams of ultrasound, notes, "The beams can make, break or rearrange molecules, control the crystalline structure of matter and even levitate objects or blobs of liquid."* As our work and that of other researchers has shown, this statement may not be limited to ultrasound; it may also be applicable to audible sound, and particularly humming. Our investigations are ongoing and evidence for this hypothesis is adding up. In the meantime, when we are asked about what sort of conditions can be healed through sound, we often repeat this line from the *Times* article and then ask: If sound can make, break, or rearrange molecules, what conditions cannot potentially be healed and transformed using sound?

---

*M. W. Browne, "Sound Is Shaped into a Dazzling Tool with Many Uses," *New York Times*, February 9, 1988.

3

Breath and Sound

Without breath, there can be no sound. Dr. Andrew Weil, noted integrative medicine expert, was once a guest on the *Dr. Oz Show*, and Dr. Oz asked him what he thought was the single most important thing people could do to improve their health. Dr. Weil answered with one word: "Breathe!" We would agree. And we would add, "Then hum!"

Please pause for a moment and take a nice, slow, deep breath. Hold your breath in for a few seconds and then slowly release it. Perhaps you might do it again. As you do, observe yourself and notice any changes that may occur.

Numerous studies have shown that deep breathing, even for just a few breaths, can have significant positive physiological effects: your heart rate slows, your blood pressure drops, and you feel more relaxed, centered, and focused. When you combine conscious breathing with humming, you amplify that relaxation response and radically reduce your level of stress.

Pranayama, or the Science of Breath

The science of breath has been the subject of many great teachings. Books have been written on the subject. It is the focal point of some yoga traditions and the basis of many esoteric body-mind-spirit practices. Many spiritual traditions consider breath to be sacred. This energy is called "prana" in the Hindu traditions. In the Orient, it is known as "chi" or "ki". In the Hebrew tradition, for example, one word for breath is *ruach*, which also means "spirit". Wilhelm Reich, Sigmund Freud's disciple, found breath a major source of the energy he called "orgone" and spent many years studying its power. This energy goes by many different names in the various cultures, countries, and spiritual paths on our planet. Yet it is the same. It is the energy of life—the energy of the breath.

In the Hindu tradition of pranayama, breath is seen as the source of *prana*, or vital energy. As you breathe in, your body takes on a charge of this energy. As you hold your breath, your body builds this charge of energy. As you release your breath, your body releases this charge of energy. This is, of course, a simplification of pranayama. Though simple, it is profound, for energy practitioners understand that when we focus our awareness on the power of breath, we can regulate and change our energetic body. (In chapter 7, we will discuss a technique called bhramari pranayama that combines deep breathing with humming.)

In terms of the proper way of breathing, there are many different schools of thought. Some people believe that proper breathing should occur only through the nose, while others hold that breathing should always occur through the mouth. Some people recommend taking an "in breath" for 4 seconds, holding it for 4 seconds, and then exhaling it for 4 seconds. Others believe that the best method is to breathe in for 8 seconds, hold for 8 seconds, and release for 8 seconds. There are endless variations What we think is important is simply that you take slow, deep breaths in whatever manner feels comfortable for you.

Without breath, we have no capacity to make sound. Whether it's a hum, a sigh, or a spoken word, our sound rides on our breath. Before we begin to talk about how to hum, we want to be sure that you are able to breathe as fully and effectively as possible. Utilizing various breathing techniques to support our sounds, such as diaphragmatic breathing, can be most helpful as we begin to work with our own self-created sounds.

Diaphragmatic Breathing

Whether you breathe in through your nose or your mouth, we suggest that you practice diaphragmatic breathing—that is, breathe into your diaphragm. The diaphragm sits just below your rib cage. When you breathe into your diaphragm, you should feel your rib cage and belly expand. This method of breathing ensures that your lungs fill to capacity as you breathe.

Diaphragmatic breathing, incidentally, is a very natural way to breathe. If you watch infants breathe, you'll see that it's what they do; their little bellies rise up and then gently relax. So even if you're not accustomed to breathing in this manner right now, remember that you once breathed this way, and you can easily learn to do it again.

Many years ago, at the end of one of our first Healing Sounds Intensive workshops—a nine-day training that we have presented for twenty-one years in Colorado to teach participants almost everything you could want to know about sound healing, from psycho-acoustics to mantras to tuning forks—a participant came up to Jonathan.

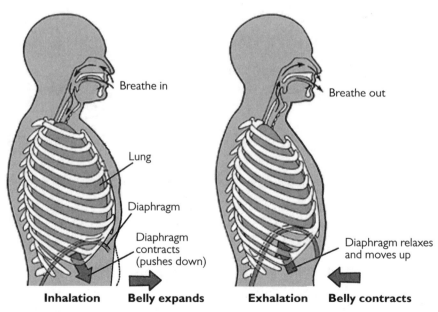

Fig. 3.1. In diaphragmatic breathing, your belly expands as you breathe in and contracts as you breathe out.

"Mr. Goldman," this man began, "I hate to bother you, but could I ask you a question?"

Jonathan stopped doing what he was doing and nodded. "Certainly," he replied. "How can I help you?"

"Well, I just can't seem to hold a note the way everyone else can," he answered.

Jonathan asked him to take a breath and then release it with a sound. He saw that the man was taking a very shallow breath. His shoulders rose, but his abdomen was still, indicating that only the tops of his lungs had expanded with air. So, over the next few minutes Jonathan taught him how to breathe diaphragmatically, with nice deep breaths. After that the man was able to make and hold a note for as long as his compatriots.

That incident was an astounding revelation to us that something as natural and simple as breathing needed to be taught. We had taken for granted that everyone—especially people who worked with sound—knew how to breathe diaphragmatically. Now, we make sure to teach diaphragmatic breathing at the beginning of every single workshop we facilitate. In fact, we think it is a good thing to review with you now.

⌒ Breathing Diaphragmatically

Many of you may remember, as we do, being shown how to breathe in school, with your shoulders raised and your stomach and rib cage remaining firm and unmoving. Such breathing is not effective in terms of expanding your lung capacity. If you take a deep breath and find that your shoulders are rising, you are most likely not breathing diaphragmatically. You may also find yourself feeling tense. If this is the case, it might be helpful to practice diaphragmatic breathing.

- Lie on your back on the floor. Place your hands on your belly.
- Breathe in, focusing your intention on bringing the air into the deepest part of your lungs and belly. Imagine that your abdomen is a balloon that you're gently blowing up. Feel your belly rise as you breathe in.

- Breathe out, feeling your belly sink and relax as the air is pushed out of your lungs.
- Repeat until this way of breathing begins to feel natural.

Congratulations! You are now practicing diaphragmatic breathing. By breathing in this manner, you are increasing the supply of oxygen to your bloodstream and giving all the organs of your body more energy. If you're interested in learning more about breathing, including how to use it in conjunction with conscious intention, there are a number of books available, such as *Conscious Breathing* by Gay Hendricks.

Toning: Practice with Self-Created Sounds

Toning describes the practice of making elongated sounds, like *Om* or *ah*. Humming is considered a type of toning. Toning is often performed with the intention of healing or entering a deep state of consciousness.

While this book is focused primarily on humming, toning with elongated vowel sounds is one of the easiest ways to begin to feel how self-created sounds can vibrate in different parts of your body. People who are just getting started with humming may find that they feel the vibrations only in the throat area. However, with practice, toning will help you become aware of how you can target different parts of your body with vibrations from different self-created sounds.

Please listen to tracks 1 and 2 of the instructional audio tracks.

⌒ Toning Practice

To practice toning, we are going to be working with three simple vowel sounds:

"ooo" (as in the word *you*)

"ah" (as in the word *ma*)

"eee" (as in the word *me*)

- Find a comfortable location where you will be able to make sound freely without being disturbed.

- Sit comfortably, with your back straight, making sure that you are not bent over.
- Begin each set of toning exercises by taking a few slow, deep diaphragmatic breaths, releasing any stress or tension in your body.

❦ Toning "Ooo"

The "ooo" sound, the first of the toning sequence, is a deep sound with very subtle vibrations. It may take some time and practice before you can feel them.

- Close your eyes. Focus your attention on your breathing. Take three slow, deep breaths, feeling your body relax.
- Make the deepest "ooo" sound that you can. Make this sound three times.
- As you make this "ooo" sound, become aware of the sound vibrating not only in your throat, but also in the lower part of your body, particularly around and below your abdomen. (If you are having trouble feeling the vibration, try lightly placing your hands on your lower abdomen.)

❦ Toning "Ah"

The second sound of this sequence is the midrange "ah" sound.

- Close your eyes. Focus your attention on your breathing. Take three slow, deep breaths, feeling your body relax.
- Make the midrange "ah" sound. Make this sound three times.
- As you make this "ah" sound, become aware of this sound vibrating not only in your throat but also in your upper chest. (If you are having trouble feeling this vibration, try lightly placing your hands on your upper chest.)

❦ Toning "Eee"

The final sound for this sequence is the highest "eee" sound that you can comfortably make.

- Close your eyes. Focus your attention on your breathing. Take three slow, deep breaths, feeling your body relax.
- Make the highest "eee" sound that you can comfortably make. Make this sound three times.

- As you make the "eee" sound, become aware of this sound vibrating not only in your throat but also in the top of your head. (If you are having trouble feeling this vibration, try lightly placing your hands on the top of your head.)

After completing all three sounds, take a moment to reexamine how you are feeling and note what you have experienced. Were you able to feel the sounds vibrating in the various parts of your body? Do you feel more relaxed now? More balanced? Was this exercise easy, or was it challenging? We ourselves find that journaling our experiences—writing down what we did, how we felt, and the effects of the exercise—is helpful, and we suggest that you have pen and paper handy so that you can record your own experiences with sound.

If you are having difficulty feeling the resonance of these sounds today, try them again at another time. The more you experiment with sound, the easier it will be to experience. You are your own best laboratory, and repeating your "experiments" and writing down your results in a journal is often very helpful as you're doing your "lab" work.

⌒ Toning from "Ah" to "Eee"

An additional exercise that you might enjoy is to go from one vowel sound to another, feeling the change in resonance in your body.

- Close your eyes. Focus your attention on your breathing. Take three slow, deep breaths, feeling your body relax.
- Place one hand on your chest and the other on the top of your head.
- Make the midrange "ah" sound and then, with the same breath, change pitch to the highest "eee" sound you can comfortably make. Feel the resonance shifting in your body.
- Repeat several times.

Please know that the experience of different sounds resonating different parts of your body is not imaginary. It is real. In fact, professional singers—particularly classically trained vocalists—will talk about having a head voice and a body voice. It's a real phenomenon and one that we trust you will experience and enjoy. It can truly open up your consciousness to a greater understanding of the power of sound.

4
Our Thoughts Matter

Sound is an exceptionally powerful energy. As we've discussed in our last few chapters, it has the ability to stimulate the release of hormones in the body, to reduce the stress response and induce relaxation, to penetrate the body and affect us at a cellular level, to rearrange molecular structure, and to shape matter itself. Our ancient cultures believed that sound was the fundamental force of creation, and perhaps they were right. Our modern scientists tell us that everything is vibration—everything is sound!

We'd now like to introduce a vital element that seems to magnify the power of our self-created sounds. As we've come to understand, frequencies are the vibrational wavelengths by which different objects resonate. Everything is said to have its own resonant frequency (or frequencies as is also believed), and reinforcing that natural resonance in the body is an important component in the therapeutic and transformational application of sound. There seems to be another component that is equally, if not more, important: intention. It seems that our intentions (or thoughts, beliefs, feelings, or purpose) can be encoded on the sounds we make to amplify their effect. Let us explain.

The Placebo Effect

The word *placebo* comes from Latin, meaning "I shall please." The placebo effect is the improvement that a patient derives from treatment that is not due to the specific treatment itself. As a simplified example, consider a clinical study of a new medication. The study subjects are, unbeknownst to them, divided into two groups. One group receives the medication, and the other group receives a placebo—a pill that looks just like the medication but has only inert ingredients. Both groups are told what the positive effects of the medication will be. Amazingly enough, some of the subjects in the placebo group will experience those positive effects, even without having taken the actual medication. Their belief will be so powerful that it affects their physical body. This is the placebo effect.

Rather than explore the powerful implications of the phenomenon, scientists largely ignored the placebo effect, considering it to be simply a factor they had to discount or circumvent in their studies. That is, until the last decade or so, when researchers began to see the significance of this effect in terms of the connection between the mind and the body.

Now the placebo effect—the power of our belief to dramatically affect and influence our physical bodies (and perhaps more)—is being vigorously investigated. Scientists, doctors, researchers, and healers are realizing that for many individuals, healing may be amplified and accelerated by their beliefs. What once was dismissed as a bothersome factor that had to be worked around in clinical trials in order to accurately gauge the effectiveness of treatment is now being seriously considered as a potent adjunct or facilitator to treatment. This new development helps validate that important component of sound healing we previously mentioned: intention.

Lesley University

We now ask you to kindly step into our time machine and travel back to the mid-1980s, when Jonathan was completing his master's degree at

Lesley University in Cambridge, Massachusetts, which focused on the therapeutic uses of sound as a healing modality. He had collected and was correlating systems of using sound for healing, and he was working on a book based on his research.

Many of these sound healing systems involved resonating the energy centers of our body, known as the chakras, with sound, and a fair number involved systems for resonating the physical organs with sound. Jonathan had been collecting this information for nearly a decade and had amassed documentation on hundreds of systems from different scientists and spiritual masters. The problem was that despite their claims of success, most of these systems did not correlate or even agree with one another. You'd have spiritual master A using one specific mantra for a particular chakra and spiritual master B using a completely different mantra for that same chakra, with both of them reporting the same beneficial results. Or they'd use the same mantra for different chakras and again have matching results. Similar issues arose with the scientists who were kind enough to share their work. Dr. X would use a certain frequency for an organ, while Dr. Y would use a completely different frequency for the same organ, and yet they would have the same beneficial results.

Jonathan comes from a family of medical doctors—his grandfather, father, and brother have all been MDs—and at the time of this research he was extremely left brained, focusing on the logical and not the intuitive. Thus, when examining the discrepancies among all these different systems, he found himself in a state of intellectual angst. How was it possible that all these different systems have the same positive results if they were not in agreement? There was too much variation among them. It made no sense.

A Life-Changing Experience

Jonathan remembers sitting in front of his computer (so long ago that it used a DOS operating system) trying to figure out how all these different systems that utilized sound for healing could coexist with one another. He simply could not understand how they could possibly be so varied and yet still all work, producing healing results. He sat with his head in his hands in immense despair.

Suddenly, Jonathan had a profound thought: "It is not only the frequency of the sound that creates the effect, it is also the intention of the person making and receiving the sound that causes the outcome." He opened his eyes and began typing the words: **"Frequency + Intent = Healing."** Those words appeared in his first book, *Healing Sounds*, as did a corollary: "Vocalization + Visualization = Manifestation." Later he came up with other variants, including "Sound + Belief = Outcome" and "Vibration + Feeling = Creation."

What exactly is intent? From our perspective, it is the consciousness (or thoughts, feelings, or visualization) that we encode upon the sounds that we make. And incidentally, whether or not we are aware of it, we encode our language with intent all the time. No doubt you've had people say to you "I love you." The intent of the words will be very different depending on whether they come from a romantic partner, a sibling, a friend, or perhaps even someone who is actually peeved with you. Think about it. The words (the sound, vibration, frequency, or whatever you want to call it) may be the same, but the energy behind the words (the intent, feeling, visualization, or whatever) is very different. And because of that encoding, the effect of the totality of the sound is also very different.

After many years of working in the field of sound healing, we have discovered that this initial formula, **Frequency + Intent = Healing**, may be one of the most important aspects of the healing nature of sound.

At the time of Jonathan's research the idea of "Intent" was virtually unheard of—particularly in the scientific community. You can substitute many other words for it—visualization, belief, feeling, purpose— no one word is sufficient since it is basically the consciousness of those making and receiving the sound that is so important with regard to the effect of the sound. At the time, the idea that our thoughts could somehow be encoded on sound and have an influence was not taken seriously by those in the scientific community. That, however, has changed. Now there are television specials on the subject of intention and a plethora of books by distinguished authors in both the scientific and medical communities.

Water Crystal Photography

One of the most visually stunning demonstrations of intention comes from the work of Dr. Masaru Emoto, a Japanese scientist who photographed water using a special "dark field" microscope (which allows the object being viewed to appear as a bright image on a dark background). Dr. Emoto would expose water to various influences, from physical contaminants like chemicals to more intangible factors like music or prayer. He would then freeze the water and photograph the resulting ice crystals.

Remarkably, Dr. Emoto found that intention carries great weight in the structuring of the ice crystals. For example, he would fill a series of jars with water and then label each jar with various words and phrases. He found that water from jars labeled with positive words like "love," "thank you," or "appreciation" transformed into beautiful, geometrically shaped snowflake-like crystals when frozen. Words with negative intent such as "I hate you" froze into mud-like structures.

Perhaps the most powerful of these images are two photographs of water from the lake at Fujiwara Dam in Japan. This water was quite polluted, and the image in the photograph looked like mud. Dr. Emoto then asked a spiritual master to chant and pray over the same water for about twenty minutes, and then he froze and photographed it again. The resultant image looked like a beautiful, geometrically perfect snowflake. These images wondrously demonstrate the combined power of sound and intention.*

---

*For those interested in viewing these and other photographs by Dr. Emoto, please visit: https://www.healingsounds.com/messages-from-water-the-work-of-masuru-emoto.

While the actual statistics vary, water comprises anywhere from 70 to 90 percent of our physical body. If a chanted prayer (which from our perspective is nothing more or less than positive sound with intent) can transform the mudlike quality of polluted water to the crystalline beauty of purified water, is this not a plausible demonstration of our formula **Frequency + Intent = Healing?**

Good Vibrations

We began this chapter talking about the placebo effect and the power of belief. There are now many scientists who are doing outstanding work with regard to validating the importance of the placebo effect. One of the most influential is Dr. Bruce Lipton. His groundbreaking book, *Biology of Belief,* is one of the most decisive works regarding the importance of belief.

Dr. Lipton writes about a study of a group of people who had been referred to a surgeon for arthroscopic knee surgery, a procedure that is utilized to reduce pain in the knee. As part of this experiment, only half the patients had the actual surgery; the other half were cut open and then stitched back up, so that it looked like they had had the surgery, even though they had not. As it turns out, both groups healed and experienced pain reduction at the same rate. Here we have a remarkable example of the placebo effect: those who believed they had had the operation healed as well as those who did have the actual operation.

Dr. Lipton also did research on a cellular level. Common theory has long held that the nucleus of a cell, which holds its genetic material, functions like a brain, governing the cell's processes and interactions. If that were true, however, then nature (heredity) would reign supreme over nurture (environment). To prove that environmental factors may be more of an influence on us than had been previously thought, Dr. Lipton decided to ennucleate cells—that is, to remove their nucleus, leaving the rest of each cell undisturbed. If the nucleus functioned as a brain, he reasoned, the ennucleated cells would quickly lose all function and die. How long would that death take? Minutes? Hours? No one had ever done this work before. As it turns out, the ennucleated cells actually survived for two months or more, and they were still able to make complex responses to environmental stimuli.

The nucleus and its genes, therefore, could not be the "brain" of the cell. Dr. Lipton continued his research, eventually establishing that the membrane of the cell was the driving force behind the cell's processes and interaction. He also determined that the membrane was highly responsive to environmental stimuli, including both physical and energetic—that is, vibrational—factors. When we asked Dr. Lipton if he thought sound could be an environmental factor that contributed to the cellular functioning, he began to sing the chorus of the Beach Boys' song "Good Vibrations" to us. That is all it is, he exclaimed—the vibrations we manifest to and for ourselves.

The Quantum Field

We would be remiss if we didn't mention the work of Dr. Joe Dispenza and his innovative book *You Are the Placebo.* Dr. Dispenza is a chiropractor and a neurologist who in his early twenties was involved in an accident that caused severe trauma to his spine. His doctors told him that if he ever wanted to walk again, he would need steel rods inserted in his spine. Joe visited numerous physicians and received the same diagnosis. But for some reason, he was guided not to undergo surgery but, instead, to heal himself.

For weeks, Joe utilized a form of visualization that helped to focus his awareness on healing the fractured vertebrae of his spine. It was apparently an arduous process, but six weeks later, he took his first step by himself and slowly began to walk. This experience led him on a journey of self-discovery, which included investigation of meditation, the brain, quantum mechanics, and "miracle" healings. This is another example of the power of intent.

For us, perhaps the most interesting aspect of Dr. Dispenza's work involves what he calls "the quantum field." We like to think of it as the unmanifested part of our potential reality—that which contains unlimited possibilities. Possibilities can then be made manifest by directing our attention to them.

Our friend and colleague Gregg Braden writes about the "observer effect" in many of his books, including *The Divine Matrix*. It seems that an electron behaves differently depending on whether or not it is being observed. When observed, the electron behaves as a particle. When left by itself in that unmanifested quantum field, it behaves as a wave.

For many, this concept is difficult to believe. How can our mere observation change the physical manifestation of an object, no matter how small? Yet the observer effect is one of the cornerstones of quantum physics. The implications are enormous, and possibly lend rationale to the remarkable idea that we have the ability to manifest reality through our thoughts and our belief system. People all around the world are teaching various techniques that enable students to do what seems to be the impossible. From our perspective, much of these seemingly miraculous abilities can be attributed to the power of intention.

Several years ago, we were about to give a workshop and were fixing a cup of tea in the kitchen of the venue. We had just poured the water and not yet turned off the stove. A friend came into the room to visit and before we were able to warn her, she leaned on the stove burner and severely burned her hand. She had been trained in several therapies that utilized quantum field theory and immediately held her hand away from her sight. We understood what she was doing—if she didn't observe her burnt hand, she could potentially restore it through visualizing her hand in the quantum field and creating it as being perfectly unscathed.

"Don't worry!" she said. "I can fix this. Just don't let me see it." And neither of us did, turning off the stove and ignoring the situation as best we could. The next day, she came back and showed us her hand. It was quite normal looking—perhaps only a slight pinkish color where the coils of the stove had burned it. Through the quantum field, she had been able to heal her hand using visualization, belief, and intent.

A Fire Walk

More than twenty-five years ago, Jonathan took part in a fire walk. An enormous bonfire had been built, and after it had been reduced down to coals, all the ashes were spread out for people to walk on. During this time, the facilitator had been giving instructions on how to fire walk (it was a six-hour workshop). These included an affirmative chant of "I can walk on fire. I can do anything!" along with a mantra, "cool moss," that the fire walkers were supposed to visualize while they walked on the hot coals.

Jonathan had not attended the workshop, but when it came time for the fire walk, he slipped into line with those who wanted to participate in walking on the fiery bed of hot coals. He walked across the coals, reciting the "cool moss" mantra, and did not get burnt. He remembers that for him the experience did not seem much out of the ordinary: "I always knew I could walk on fire. And I did." However, his friend who did the fire walk had a different experience. "On my third step," his friend said, "I thought, 'I can't be doing this!' and I got a blister that covered my entire foot!"

This seems like an early example of the power of intent—the positive or negative ability of belief to creates an outcome.

Quantum Sound

We have given you scientific explanations for many aspects of healing, like transmitting the correct resonant frequency into the body to strengthen it, or using a frequency to shatter cancer cells. Certainly these methods are all viable and helpful. But from our perspective, there is more. Much more. Our thoughts can delve into the quantum soup of unmanifested reality and cause the sound that we create to have very unique abilities. Depending upon our intention, the sound we create can have very different effects. Indeed, the **"Frequency + Intent = Healing"** concept may hold the secret to how any vibratory source may be used to heal.

We will soon turn specifically to the hum, which may be the most potent of all tones to be utilized in quantum sound. In particular, the power of the hum seems to be particularly resplendent in terms of obeying the intention that we give it. It is an extraordinary sound for manifestation.

Recently both of us had sore throats. We closed our eyes and began humming. While we hummed, we focused our intent on the sound resonating and healing the part of our throat that hurt. As we hummed, we visualized a white light bombarding the cells of our throat. As the humming vibrated the cells in our throat, perhaps they boosted circulation, bringing more oxygen to them. Or perhaps the vibrations caused the cells to release nitric oxide. Or perhaps any of the other physiological benefits we mentioned in chapter 1 came into being. And perhaps some quantum effect was happening that was beyond our current level of understanding. Regardless, when we were done humming, the pain in our throats was gone.

It is quite possible that, while we were humming, we could have thought of something entirely different than healing our throat, and still the pain might have gone away. However, we have spent too many years working with sound—especially self-created sound—not to know that something special occurs when you combine both frequency and intent. Quantum sound manifests the outcome more rapidly and more powerfully than simply by making the sound without intention. But in order to believe this, you will probably need to experience it yourself. And in order to experience this phenomenon, you will need to go on to our next chapter, in which we begin to work with techniques that allow you to experience the power of humming.

Before we move on, a final few words. And it seems fitting to place these words at the end of this chapter. We bring your awareness to them because we believe they are of extreme importance with regard to the power of prayer and meditation.

There is a reason why almost all the prayers on this planet are vocalized—whispered, chanted, read aloud, spoken, or sung. It is this: Sound amplifies the power of prayer. Prayer amplifies the power of sound. Together, sound and prayer (intention, thought, belief) build a mutually reinforcing feedback loop. It is that simple and that important!

PART II

Practice Makes Perfect

5
How to Hum
Getting Started at Humming

In the first part of this book we discussed sound and the various elements necessary for sound to exist, such as breath. We also talked about what may be one of the most important factors that can amplify the power of sound: intent.

In this next section, we begin to work with exercises that involve humming, starting off quite simply and then getting more advanced. We recommend that you work through these exercises in the order in which they are presented in this book. To learn any new technique, even one as innate to humans as humming, it's important to proceed step by step. It is not a race but rather a journey, and each step of the journey has its own lesson to teach.

The exercises in this book will help you gain more and more experience with sound. With each exercise and each step in the process of learning to hum, you will become more and more adept at resonating your body with sound and better able to understand and use the power of your own self-created sounds.

Since deciding to write this book, we have spent more and more time humming. Sometimes we hum by ourselves. Sometimes we hum together. It doesn't matter. Each time we hum, it is a powerful and healing experience. It is also a learning experience, because each time we hum, it is slightly different, depending on our pitch, our intention, and other factors. We will discuss all these influential factors as we progress through our practice of humming.

Feel the Vibrations

Perhaps the most important aspect of humming is the actual vibrations that occur within our body as we hum. But people don't usually notice these vibrations. Often people hum a tune or a song unconsciously; when they happen to notice it, what draws their attention is usually the sound, not the feeling of vibrations.

As you begin to practice humming, we ask that you start by paying attention to feeling the sound in your body. Humming creates a lot of vibrations. As we'll discuss later, you can learn to project these vibrations to different parts of your body. As your technique progresses, you will also learn to encode intention onto your hum, further amplifying its power. This will build your hum into a vibrational tool for physical, emotional, mental, and spiritual transformation.

First, though, it's important simply to feel where the natural resonance of the hum occurs in your body as you're making the sound. In order to do this, we want to make sure that you're making a proper hum. No doubt you're quite sure you already know how to hum, but please do bear with us and read this next section regardless. If nothing else, we trust you'll find it amusing and fun to read. And you might even learn something from it.

You Know How to Whistle

How many of you are familiar with the classic movie *To Have and Have Not*? It was a 1944 American film starring Humphrey Bogart and Lauren Bacall. Whether or not you have actually seen the movie, you may know a line from it that's become so famous that it made it to #34 on the American Film Institute's list of the top hundred greatest movie quotes of all time.

In this particular scene, Lauren Bacall and Humphrey Bogart are flirting with each other. Bacall says to Bogart's character, Steve: "You know how to whistle, don't you, Steve? You just put your lips together and blow." Now, this quote may not be as famous as Shakespeare's "to be or not to be," but we think it's a fun way to demonstrate the beginning of our humming lessons.

If you've ever tried to teach a child how to whistle, you know it can be difficult. We've met some adults who still have not perfected their whistle. On the other hand, there are professional whistlers who get paid a good salary in Hollywood for their whistling ability (just listen to the theme song from *The Good, the Bad and the Ugly* and you'll hear one of the most famous melodies in modern music, being whistled by a professional).

Despite Bacall's memorable line, whistling is not necessarily as simple as putting your lips together and blowing through them. But can the same thing be said about humming? Is there anyone on this planet who can vocalize sound but not hum? We think not. We think that everyone, from newborn babies to the very elderly, can hum. Whether or not they can speak, sing, tone, or what have you, they can undoubtedly hum. It is a universal sound.

The Nose Must Be Open

In the 1950s, when we were still adolescents, Random House published a series of "All About" books. They were science books covering a variety of subjects and meant for juvenile readers. Most were written by experts in the field who just happened to think that kids deserved to know something about the subjects they themselves knew so much about. It's said that Einstein once stated that if you really knew something about a subject, you could explain it to a child. The "All About" books attempted to do just that (and we ourselves have attempted to continue that tradition in our own field of sound, taking complicated research on sound and simplifying it so that even people who are not as fascinated with the subject as we are can understand it).

We remember reading *All About Dinosaurs, All About Whales, All About Reptiles, All About Stars*, and a number of other books in this series. They were truly excellent books that we both enjoyed. A couple of years ago, a friend gave us a book called *All About Sound* that was part of this series. Neither of us had read it. We were thrilled.

We'd like to say that we discovered a lot that day reading *All About Sound*, but by then we knew most of the material regarding sound. But we did learn one thing that was so profoundly simple and yet so powerful that we found ourselves stunned. It was this: the book suggested that we hum and then hold our nostrils shut and see what happens. So, we hummed and pinched our nostrils closed. And something amazing happened: the sound stopped.

It had never occurred to us to try this before. We were giddy with glee. We did it again and the same thing happened. Since then, whenever we mention the subject of humming to people, we inevitably ask them to hum while holding their nostrils shut. The result for us is usually pretty funny, because we've yet to encounter anyone who has already known that you can't hum when your nose is blocked. We've explored this sonic prank many times with some very experienced professional people in the field of sound healing. Some have written books on sound for healing and transformation. Others have devised instruments that are used for sound healing. Still others are expert teachers on sound. None had any idea. Actually, there was one person who knew about the nose and humming. It was the person who had given us *All About Sound*.

You can't hum if your nose is blocked. This was a revelation to us and a fact we share with you, as it is important with regard to proper humming. In fact, not only must your nose (and sinus cavity) be open, but in order to hum most effectively, it is considered necessary by most vocal experts to have your mouth closed as well. There are some varying opinions about this, but for our purposes, we ask that you keep your mouth closed, making sure that no air escapes from your lips when doing the humming exercises in this book.

Nearly twenty years ago, Jonathan became fascinated with Tibetan deep voice chanting. This is the extraordinarily powerful sound made by Tibetan lamas—very deep and otherworldly sounding, almost like a growl. Jonathan spent quite some time attempting to produce this unique vocal sound, but to no avail. He even attempted trying to hum and whistle at the same time. While that made quite an interesting sound, it certainly was not the Tibetan deep voice. In fact, because his mouth needed to be open in order to whistle, it wasn't even a real hum.

Several years later, Jonathan did in fact receive the Tibetan deep voice in a process he calls "harmonic transmission." He had recorded a group of Tibetan monks chanting, and he took this recording home and went to sleep meditating to the deep voice chanting of the monks. The next morning, when he woke up, he had the voice. It was a most extraordinary experience and one Jonathan still cannot explain. We wanted to include it in this book as yet another example of the seemingly unbelievable experiences that can occur through sound.

How to Hum

We've looked up various definitions of the word *hum* on the Internet and most suggest a nasal sound with lips closed. A few sites included an open mouth technique, but from our perspective, this wouldn't be a true hum—like Jonathan's experience trying to hum and whistle at the same time, open-mouth humming can produce a great sound and can be powerful, but it is not a true hum. If you open your mouth as you hum, the volume of the sound you are making increases, but the feeling of the sound vibrating usually fades. Of course, some people find that having their mouth open when they hum does not make much of a difference in the resonance they feel, but for others the difference is tremendous. We don't know if there's such a word as "pseudo-hum," but we're using it now to describe any sort of sound that has air escaping through the mouth.

At this preliminary stage of learning to hum, we ask that you hum with your lips gently closed. As you hum, you'll be able to feel your lips, throat, cheeks, and your sinus cavity vibrating. Together, these areas form your vocal cavity, and it becomes a resonating chamber as you hum. As you progress with your humming in the exercises in this book, you'll begin to be able to feel the resonance in your head and your chest as well. Ultimately, you'll be able to project a hum anywhere in your body.

For this first level of humming, let's follow the lead of Lauren Bacall and say, "You know how to hum, don't you? Just close your mouth and make a sound—and make sure you're not holding your nose!"

Choosing a Comfortable Pitch

As we discussed in chapter 2, frequency is the number of cycles per second at which a sound is vibrating. Another word for this is *pitch*. Pitch is generally a more subjective term and open to interpretation. You might, for example, note that a sound is vibrating at 100 Hz (cycles per second), and that is its frequency. But you might also simply say that it has a low pitch (a lower sound).

As we advance in our humming techniques, we will start exploring the ways in which different frequencies affect us by lowering and raising our pitch. But regardless of whatever pitch you choose to create, you don't want to strain your vocal chords. You'll know if you're straining because, quite simply, you'll feel discomfort around your throat area. Perhaps our only caveat with regard to self-created sound is to make sure that you are comfortable and relaxed. Keeping your pitch within your comfort zone is important. For most people, that means keeping their humming within the range of their normal speaking voice.

Jonathan's father was a well-known otolaryngologist (ear-nose-throat doctor) who treated many celebrities. One of these was Frank Sinatra, who once, after many evenings of singing at a New York City nightclub, strained his voice so badly that he literally lost it. He couldn't make a sound. Dr. Irving B. Goldman's prescription for this famous singer: six weeks of silence. Not even talking was allowed. After those long six weeks, Sinatra was fine (and knew enough to rest his voice when necessary). He was not unique, however. Numerous singers have managed to strain their vocal chords and had to rest in order to heal.

With regard to making comfortable self-created sound, we also ask you to remember that louder is not better. Particularly when you are working with humming for health and wellness, the most effective and comfortable sounds are not particularly loud at all. Sound does not need to be loud in order to create resonance or vibration.

While this book is dedicated to the healing and transformative use of humming, we must acknowledge that anything that can be used positively can also have the opposite effect. From our perspective, humming has only positive and beneficial experiences—as long as you are gentle with yourself and don't overdo it.

So once again we begin with, "You know how to hum, don't you?" And now add: "Just close your mouth and make a comfortable sound."

Please listen to track 3 of the instructional audio tracks.

⌢ Beginning to Hum

The most basic hum begins with the "mmmmm" sound. Pretend you've taken a bite of the most delicious food you've ever had, and with a comfortable and gentle voice, make a sound that shows your appreciation: "mmmmmmm." That's the hum.

As they learn to hum, people occasionally have slight difficulty initially making this sound. If that's the case for you, you might try starting instead with the well-known mantra *Om,* closing your lips after the "oh" and drawing out the "mmmmm." You could also start with the actual word *hum,* closing your lips after the "huh" and elongating the "mmmmm."

As you hum, some proponents suggest that your jaw should be relaxed and that it's not necessary for your teeth to be touching. Others say that the teeth be gently touching. We've even encountered sources that call for clenching your teeth. Personally, for ourselves, we keep our mouth closed and our lower jaw as relaxed as possible. Depending upon your oral cavity, this might mean having a slight space between your upper and lower teeth, or it could mean having your the teeth rest lightly against each other. We do not recommend clenching your teeth—we have found a relaxed jaw is best when you are humming for health and wellness.

- Find a comfortable location where you will be able to make sound freely without being disturbed.
- Sit comfortably with your back straight, making sure that you are not bent over. It's possible to hum while you are lying down, but the vibrational effect that we are seeking will not be the same. You could also hum while standing, but when we stand, a certain portion of our mind is occupied with balance and dealing with gravity. Sitting up is the best position for using self-created sound for healing and transformation. In addition, it is helpful to have your eyes closed when making vocalized sound. This seems to amplify the ability to feel the resonance of the hum.
- Take a few slow, deep diaphragmatic breaths, releasing any stress or tension in your body.
- Take one more slow, deep breath and then gently hum, using the *mmmmm, Om,* or *hum* sound, as described above. If you are using the *Om* or *hum* sound, spend only a second or two with the initial "oh" or "huh" and then use the rest of your breath for the "mmmmm."
- Hum in a monotone, holding the same tone throughout, without varying your pitch. Hold the hum for five to ten seconds, or as long as is comfortable. Do not overextend the hum to the point of discomfort.
- When your hum ends, take one or more deep diaphragmatic breaths, and then hum again. Practice making the sound, keeping your pitch steady, and keeping your volume gentle until you feel comfortable with your hum.

⌢ Feeling the Vibrations

For this exercise we suggest that you allow at least fifteen minutes—five minutes for humming, five minutes for relaxation, and five minutes for grounding.

Please limit your actual humming to about five minutes; you can set a timer for yourself or just limit yourself to approximately twenty-five humming sounds, which generally takes about five minutes. Either method is fine.

- Take a few slow, deep diaphragmatic breaths, releasing any stress or tension in your body.
- Now begin to hum. As you hum, focus on where in your body you are feeling the sound. You are likely to feel the vibrations somewhere in the region of your vocal cavity, your skull, or even your chest, but there is no one right place to be feeling the hum at this point. You may be surprised to find that the sound is vibrating in a number of different places. Continue to hum for five minutes.
- When you have finished humming, remain seated in silence with your eyes closed for five minutes or so, continuing to breathe slowly and deeply. Check yourself out. How are you feeling? You may be feeling light-headed. Perhaps a part of your body that was in discomfort is feeling better. Thanks to the physiological benefits of self-created sound, you may be feeling calm and relaxed.
- When you feel ready, open your eyes. Begin to ground yourself, bringing your awareness back to your surroundings. Perhaps you'll want to wiggle your toes or your fingers, as this can help you feel yourself back in your body. Once you feel fully present (and not at all light-headed or woozy), you can get up.

While you were humming, were you able to focus your attention and become aware of the vibration of your hum? Where did you feel it? Was it vibrating your sinuses or the top of your mouth? Or perhaps you were feeling the vibration in your throat or maybe your teeth? Where were you feeling the sound? Cultivating that awareness may be the most important element of your initial humming experience, as it is necessary that you consciously feel the vibration of the hum in order to use it for healing and transformation. So, for this specific exercise our main purpose was simply for you to begin to feel the vibrations of your hum. That is all. Yet we must acknowledge that some physical and emotional effects can occur. We have even seen people fall asleep while doing this exercise. That's fine.

Remember, it's important to give yourself plenty of time after humming for relaxing and grounding, which will help you assimilate your experience. And you probably don't want to plan any rigorous activities afterward. You may be too relaxed to take part in them.

Please listen to track 4 of the instructional audio tracks.

⌒ Changing Pitch

The purpose of this exercise is to give you experience humming in different pitches and detecting the sometimes subtle vibrational changes they create. You change your pitch by lowering or raising the tone of your voice, going from a low note to a higher one or from a high note to a lower one.

If you're wondering how to do this, just remember the "Do-Re-Mi" song from the movie *Sound of Music*. As you sing the notes of the scale in that song—do, re, mi, fa, so, la, ti, do—you are changing pitch. Please be aware that it is not necessary for you to be able to sing this complete scale, or to sing it well, when you begin to change your pitch. Even a very slight change in pitch is adequate for this exercise. The point is to feel the change in vibration that a change in pitch produces. It does not have to be a drastic change.

- Take a few slow, deep diaphragmatic breaths, releasing any stress or tension in your body.
- Begin to hum at a comfortable pitch, making sure it is a relaxed and gentle sound.
- When you feel ready, hum five times at your starting pitch, feeling the resonance in your body.
- Now experiment a little with your hum. Try to hit a pitch that is slightly lower than that of your starting hum. Hum this pitch about five times and feel the resonance. It will be a bit more of a bass tone, and you'll no doubt feel this sound slightly differently than the last hum.

- Return to the approximate pitch of your starting hum and hum five times.
- Now try raising your pitch a bit. It really doesn't matter what the exact note is as long as it is comfortable for you. Hum at this higher pitch five times, focusing your awareness on where you feel these sounds in your body.
- When you have finished humming, remain seated in silence with your eyes closed for five minutes or so, continuing to breathe slowly and deeply. Check yourself out. How are you feeling? You may be feeling light-headed. Perhaps a part of your body that was in discomfort is feeling better. You may be feeling calm and relaxed. Allow yourself the wonderment of this state of being—most of us are so stressed out that enjoying a relaxed state can be very healing.
- When you feel ready, open your eyes. Begin to ground yourself, bringing your awareness back to your surroundings. If you like, wiggle your toes or your fingers, as this can help you feel yourself back in your body. Once you feel fully present (and not at all light-headed or woozy), you can get up.

Perception of sound—feeling the resonance of the hum—is a skill that comes naturally for many people. For others, it may take a few attempts to be able to differentiate between the pitches. As you are experimenting with your hums, give yourself ample time for your "lab work." However, don't overdo it. You'll appreciate and enjoy them more. We suggest that you practice these beginning exercises only once a day. More is not better.

⌒ Humming a Song

This exercise, like the other exercises in this chapter, allows you to experience the resonance of different hums in your body. But it can be a more engaging way of practicing, since it calls for an activity that you've probably done many times—though you may not have been conscious of the resonance of the sound while you were doing it.

- Take a few slow, deep diaphragmatic breaths, releasing any stress or tension in your body.

- Begin to hum a song. It can be any song, or perhaps just a part of the song. A children's nursery rhyme can work well. Or you can make up your own song, humming any tune that feels good. It doesn't really matter—what is important is to feel the difference in the resonance as you hum. Hum the song for five minutes.
- At the end of five minutes, as you did for the other exercises, check yourself out and see how you are feeling. Relax. Enjoy the space you are in.
- Allow another five minutes to ground yourself, bringing your awareness to your surroundings and coming back into your body.

When you bring your attention to the vibrations of your humming, you begin to cultivate a new awareness of your body and its relationship to sound. You may have been humming all your life, but you may not have understood, until now, how the various notes in a song can vibrate different parts of your body. As always, there are no right or wrong notes when you are humming in this manner.

Summary

Please take your time when doing these exercises. They may seem simple, but the exploration of the power of sound is an eye-opening experience. It is not the destination but rather the journey that matters. You may find that you might want to spend a week or perhaps even weeks working with these exercises. And you may find that each time you do them, your experience is different.

As we begin to become aware of the resonance of the different vibrations of the sounds we hum, we become more attuned to sounds. As we become more sensitive and begin to feel the sounds resonate in our bodies, our ability to use the self-created sounds of humming for health and happiness becomes more and more active and powerful. The more attuned your sensitivity and the greater your ability to feel the sound, the more effective these exercises and the activity of humming will be for you.

If possible, keep a notebook and pen nearby while you are doing these and all the other exercises in this book. Write down any thoughts or experiences you may have. We find journaling after humming to be helpful in remembering your experience of sounding and it is something that we both highly recommend.

In our next chapter, you will experience the power of the hum in more advanced exercises. In the meantime, remember the primary exercises in this chapter. And keep humming!

6
Encoding Intent
Intermediate Humming

In this chapter we will focus on adding the power of intention to the hum. We like to think of this as conscious humming. You may find that this added component greatly increases your ability to feel the vibrations of sound in your body, as well as enhancing the healing power of your hum.

As we noted in chapter 4, in our discussion of the formula **Frequency + Intent = Healing**, in using sound for healing, we have experienced that intent is as important as the actual sound you create. And while we're using the term *intent*, you could just as easily substitute the word *belief, purpose, visualization, feeling,* or any of a multitude of other terms that mean similar things.

Unique Vibratory Beings

Our dilemma with instructing you in how to actually encode intent onto sound is this: we are all unique vibratory beings, and what works for one person does not necessarily work for another. Some people are visual, and some people are kinesthetic. For some hearing is the greatest vehicle they possess for sensing. For others it is something else. In our workshops we often ask if anyone is allergic to penicillin. And indeed, usually anywhere from 5 to 20 percent of our participants are allergic. After we take a quick count of those who are allergic to penicillin, we say, "Well, if everything is in a state of vibration and can be construed as a frequency, then that includes penicillin. It looks like between 80 and 95 percent of you will find penicillin's frequency quite healing, but it also looks like between 5 and 20 percent of you will find it toxic and potentially deadly."

We then go on to discuss the fact that no substance has the same effect on everyone; whether it is a sound, food, smell, or color, each of us reacts to it in our own way. This is a wonderful example of the fact that we are all unique vibratory beings, and that no one vibration or frequency affects everyone the same way.

This same factor seems to also apply when encoding intention on sound. Some people can simply encode a specific purpose on a sound and voilà, there it is, floating on the waveform. Others aren't able to do this. Some people may find it easiest and most effective to visualize intent as a color carried by sound. Others may work best by seeing complex geometries in their mind and projecting them onto a sound. Still others are excellent at focusing a specific feeling or emotion on a sound—they can project happiness, sadness, joy, or gratitude with extraordinary ease.

How to Encode Intent: Techniques

We cannot give you specific instructions on the very best technique to use to program intention onto the sound, but we can say with confidence to do what feels right for you and what works the best. We will describe below some of the techniques that we have found to be effective. In general, we believe that the more relaxed you are, and the more you utilize whatever modality works bests for you, the more effective you will be in the process of encoding intention.

We try to place as few limitations as possible on the practice of humming. From our perspective, having some fluidity in your practice—being able to choose whichever method works best for you at any point—helps empower you with your own innate capability of utilizing intent. We trust in the spirit of the sound to give you the experience that will be for your highest benefit in the moment.

Encoding with Gratitude and Thanks

Our esteemed colleague Gregg Braden has noted that if purely visualizing or imagining something worked for everybody, then affirmations would be a lot more successful. As powerful as our belief is, our doubts are equally powerful. Stating an affirmation that does not resonate with your inner belief is not going to do a lot of good. For example, if you don't believe that you are deserving of "meeting the partner of your dreams," or some other affirmative belief, that affirmation is not going to be very successful in manifesting your desire.

In Braden's book *The Isaiah Effect*, he emphasizes the power of feeling and visualizing an intention as though it has already happened, and then giving thanks for it. From his perspective, gratitude and appreciation lead to manifestation. Feeling a sense of gratefulness activates the electromagnetic field of the heart, which opens up the flow of positive energy.* We believe that this method—feeling our intention as though it has already happened and giving thanks—is an exceptionally potent way to encode intention onto a sound.

Dr. Joe Dispenza agrees. In his book *You Are the Placebo,* he points out that when you are expressing gratitude for something, you act as though it has already happened. Expressing gratitude for the manifestation of an intention is powerful and effective when we want to begin resonating energetically in a beneficial manner. This is quite important to remember when we are humming.

Along these same lines, the people at HeartMath Institute focus

---

*For more information on this topic see: Rollin McCraty, Ph.D., "The Energetic Heart: Bioelectromagnetic Communication within and between People," in *Clinical Applications of Bioelectromagnetic Medicine,* ed. P. J. Rosch and M. S. Markov, 541–562 (New York: Marcel Dekker, 2004).

on the energy of appreciation in the area of the heart as part of a technique that builds heart-brain coherence. Heart-brain coherence occurs when our brain waves and the rhythms of our heart synchronize.[*] This is an aspect of entrainment, which we discussed previously (see page 24). The focus on appreciation is also an example of the power of intention. Heart-brain coherence seems to amplify the electromagnetic field of the heart and make it greater than that of the brain. Some say that this form of entrainment makes the electromagnetic field of the heart fifty times stronger than the brain's field. Others estimate that the field becomes as much as five hundred to even five thousand times stronger.[†] Whatever the actual numbers might be, there is definitely an amplification process that occurs when the heart and the brain are in coherence. This is a great technique for opening up the positive flow of energy. HeartMath Institute has even developed a portable battery-operated device that teaches people how to achieve heart-brain coherence.

Our beloved mentor, Sarah "Saruah" Benson, shared with us many years ago something that continues to resonate with us to this day. It is this: "The true sound of healing is love." And indeed, if there were one thing that could be encoded upon sound that we could recommend wholeheartedly, it would be the energy of love.

However, the concept of encoding and projecting love can be challenging, since there are many different meanings and understandings of the word *love*. Some people may have had unpleasant experiences in the realm of love and thus have had great difficulty in working with this specific term. We have found that simply allowing the thoughts and feelings of appreciation to come to mind can be quite helpful in a positive and beneficial frequency.

---

[*] Y. Ma and R. McCraty, "Heart Rate Variability in Mind-Body Interventions," *Complementary Therapies in Medicine* 29 (2016): A1–A2.

[†] Rollin McCraty, Ph.D., "The Energetic Heart: Bioelectromagnetic Communication within and between People," in *Clinical Applications of Bioelectromagnetic Medicine.*

Encoding with Visualization

At its simplest, visualization calls for using your imagination, but there are basic techniques that can make visualization more powerful. To begin, it's been suggested that the most effective visualizations involve as many of the five senses (vision, touch, smell, hearing, and taste) as possible.* Keep in mind that the more you practice visualization, the better you become at it.

Some recent scientific studies have shown that people who visualize doing an activity, though they may be sitting with their eyes closed, seemed to activate that portion of the brain associated with the activity.† After these visualization, their body seems to have achieved a similar workout as if they had actually done the activity. Does this mean we may no longer have to go to the gym in order to tone our body? Probably not, but as the authors of *Scientific Visualization: Techniques and Applications* note, many athletes and musicians visualize their performances as an additional form of practice, and this seems to help them get better at what they are doing.‡

When to Encode Intent: The Still Point

We are sometimes asked about the best time to program intention onto a sound. We found one answer to that question in a book by scientist Itzhak Bentov, *Stalking the Wild Pendulum,* that suggested that there is a "still point between the in-breath and the out-breath," and that this still point is the most effective time to encode intention. So, before

---

*See Shakti Gawain, *Creative Visualization: Use the Power of Your Imagination to Create What You Want in Your Life,* 25th anniversary ed. (Novato, Calif.: New World Library, 2002).

†M. Brouziyne and C. Molinaro, "Mental Imagery Combined with Physical Practice of Approach Shots for Golf Beginners," *Perceptual and Motor Skills* 101, no. 1 (2005): 203–11; A. R. Isaac, "Mental Practice—Does it Work in the Field?" *The Sport Psychologist* 6 (1992): 192–98; and K. A. Martin and C. R. Hall, "Using Mental Imagery to Enhance Intrinsic Motivation," *Journal of Sport and Exercise Psychology* 17, no. 1 (1995): 54–69.

‡K. W. Brodlie, L. A. Carpenter, R. A. Earnshaw, J. R. Gallop, R. J. Hubbold, A. M. Mumford, C. D. Osland, and P. Quarendon, eds. (Springer Verlag, 1992).

humming, take a deep breath, and in the moment when you are holding your breath before you release it, try using that still point space to encode the intention before making your sound.

We have taught this placement of intention at the still point of the breath at our sound healing workshops. For some people it has worked well. Nevertheless, as we continue with our concept of embodying fluidity in our teachings, we encourage you to experiment with this technique and to also do what feels most natural and comfortable for you.

The Next Step: What to Encode

What will your intention be? The possibilities are limitless. You might, for example, hum with the intention of pain reduction, relaxation, sleep enhancement, alleviation of depression, stimulation of healing, an inner massage, treatment of headaches, feeling peace, experiencing happiness, and innumerable other effects that you might want to achieve. No doubt, if there's something in your life you want to change or manifest, you can project your intention of it while you are humming. It all depends on what is most appropriate for you at the time.

Is there a part of your body that's giving you discomfort? That would be an ideal place to project the intention of healing. Are you feeling stressed out and need a bit of chill? What an excellent time to hum for relaxation. Tossing and turning in bed, unable to sleep? Research has shown that five minutes of humming while you're lying in bed is highly effective in enhancing sleep. (We are aware that we've recommended that while humming you sit with your back straight in a chair, but if you're in bed and trying to sleep, we're not going to ask you to get out of your bed and go find a chair to hum in. Stay in bed. Remember, it's important to have fluidity in your practice.)

As we have been working more and more with our own humming while writing this book, we have found that if we spend a brief time taking some slow, deep breaths, our purpose or intention for humming usually comes into our consciousness. Oftentimes we have a very specific purpose—maybe we simply want to relax, or maybe we have a stuffed nose that we'd like to clear, or a headache we'd like to relieve.

Speaking of a headache, when you're humming, your skull (and obviously your brain) will be naturally vibrating. If you have a headache, try targeting the area in your head where you feel the pain with humming sounds while focusing your intention on relieving the discomfort. You may be startled at how quickly you feel the resonance inside your head. You might be amazed at what happens.

A Quick Review

In chapter 3, we had you tone three different vowel sounds ranging from deep to midrange to high notes. You undoubtedly experienced different resonances in your body as you performed the exercise; usually the low sounds will resonate the lower part of your abdominal cavity, the midrange sounds will resonate the chest area, and the high sounds will resonate the head. This exercise was to help you realize that your self-created sounds can resonate different parts of your body and can truly change the way you perceive your own sounds.

In chapter 5, we went through several exercises that allowed you to feel the vibrations of your hum. With the first exercise, you simply hummed on a monotone. Then you hummed and focused on becoming aware of the vibrations in your body. Next you worked with slightly shifting the pitch of your hum. Then you hummed a song in order to feel the variance in vibrations.

Now we are going to add the special ingredient of intent in order to bring to you the experience of conscious humming. All of the factors we have been through in those earlier exercises can influence the experience. When you couple aspects of humming such as pitch with the intention of where you'd like the sound to go in your body, you might be very surprised at the outcome. Got a sore hip? Just make a tone and play with the pitch a bit—perhaps lowering it just a little while you encode the sound with the intent of resonating your hip. Then, as you're humming and sending this intention to your hip, try adding another intention to your hum (we never said you could only project one intention at a time). You might try visualizing a golden white light that is soothing and healing flowing to your hip as you're humming. This, of course, is just an example of what one person might do. As we've said, the possibilities are limitless. Humming while encoding intention on the sound is a powerful way to assist in learning how to project sound to different parts of your body.

While you're humming, the specific physiological effects we discussed earlier will also be occurring. They include:

- Increased oxygen in the cells
- Lowered blood pressure and heart rate
- Increased lymphatic circulation
- Increased levels of melatonin
- Reduced levels of stress-related hormones
- Release of endorphins—biochemical opiates that work as natural pain relievers
- Increased levels of nitric oxide, a molecule associated with the promotion of healing
- Release of oxytocin, the "trust hormone"

Intention and Humming

As students of both science and spirituality, we understand on a deep level that sound by itself is extremely potent. When the aspect of intention is added, some truly extraordinary things can occur. But before we give instructions on the specific exercises, we'd like to share a few more thoughts about intention.

From personal experience, when we've had a pain or discomfort—in our head or anywhere in our body—and we've focused the attention of our hum to that area, often (and usually quite surprisingly) that discomfort will disappear or at least lessen. That relief might come from the release of nitric oxide, the production of endorphins, a relaxation response, or some other physiological factor. There's no doubt that these physiological benefits occur. However, from our own experience, we understand that the intention placed upon the sound is a crucial component. Something powerful and important occurs when we hum with conscious intention.

As we've mentioned, the possibilities of conditions that can be positively affected with intention when you are humming are endless. Sometimes, we hum to generate better blood flow to our tissues. Other times, we may be feeling stressed out and take a few minutes to hum and calm down. We literally visualize the humming going throughout our entire body as we're making the sound. No doubt all the physical effects of the hum contribute to this, but we know that the intention we produce and encode upon the sound is also affecting the outcome.

As we have mentioned, the possible ways in which you can encode your intention on your sound are seemingly limitless, for conscious humming is limited only by your consciousness. For example, you might have a pain in a certain part of your body and envision an angel or some other divine entity putting healing energy into that area. Or you might visualize encoding all your cells with vitality, dissipating any imbalanced energy. We've known people who have done all sorts of seemingly miraculous things coupling intention with sound.

An application of humming that we have only briefly mentioned is the ability of the hum to act as an internal massage, affecting all the cells in the area of your body where the hum is being directed. Just as there are numerous machines on the market that create external vibrations and help soothe parts of your body where you're having discomfort, humming seems to be able to also do this naturally. Humming can do this internally, and can reach places that many of these massage devices cannot. The positive benefits of this are obvious, including the resonance of our internal cells due to their being vibrated with sound. This can create many of the effects of sound that we've noted before: oxygenating the cells and causing the release of many beneficial hormones and chemicals.

Numerous energy medicine practitioners, including well-known doctors such as Ann Marie Chiasson, M.D., in her book *Energy Healing* (Sounds True, 2011), believe energy that is blocked causes imbalances and illness in the body. Vibrations such as self-created sound cause the movement and dispersal of this blocked energy, which assists in the healing process. Once you've gained the ability to add intention to the part of your body that needs the sound, you'll find it easier to project sound to this area. Humming will then become a truly powerful healing tool.

Often we have a specific purpose when we begin humming—perhaps it's to direct the hum to a stiffness we are feeling in our neck. We hum and project our sound to that area of the body. The results can be wonderful! At other times we hum with no specific intent at all. We simply trust that the sound we are making will do whatever is best for us. Perhaps that is an intent unto itself.

Please listen to track 5 of the instructional audio tracks.

⌒ Humming Up and Down Your Spine

One of the first humming exercises Jonathan ever experienced was over thirty-five years ago with master teacher Dr. John Beaulieu. For this exercise Dr. Beaulieu gave the direction to "hum up and down your spine." This can be a fun exercise to experiment with, and it is useful for learning how both pitch and intention can affect the resonance of sound. Through projecting both pitch and intention as you hum, it becomes quite easy to literally feel the sound of the hum going up and down your spine. This exercise is very useful when learning to project your hum to different parts of the body.

There are many ways of doing this exercise. Some people will hum from the top of their head to the base of their spine in just one breath. Some will glide from one pitch to the next quite effortlessly. Others will find that doing this exercise in a slow and methodical manner is best for them. However you choose to proceed, know that you can hum up and down your body with very little vocal range; you don't need a big change in pitch. If you somehow end up doing this exercise in a group, you'll probably feel like a bunch of kids in kindergarten. Whether you're in a group or by yourself, be ready to abandon all sense of poise and pride and return to a childlike sense of wonder and adventure. No one ever said that you had to be serious when you're humming. Throw caution to the wind and simply have a fun experience. Among other things, it will assist in your ability to hum in a relaxed way.

For this exercise we suggest that you allow fifteen minutes—five minutes for humming, five minutes for relaxation, and five minutes for grounding. Please limit your actual humming to about five minutes.

- Close your eyes and take a few slow, deep diaphragmatic breaths, releasing any stress or tension in your body. As you're breathing in this manner, check yourself out—tune in and sense how you're feeling.
- When you feel ready, begin humming, remembering to make sure that you feel comfortable and that you're not straining your voice in any way. Begin with a relatively high-pitched hum as you will be progressively lowering your pitch as you move down the spine.
- Focus your awareness at the top of your head. Try to feel the vibration there.
- With each hum, slightly lower your pitch, while at the same time feeling the vibration of the sound moving from the top of your head down your spine.
- As you get to the deepest hum that you can comfortably make, feel this sound at the base of your spine. Spend a few minutes humming and experiencing this resonance.
- Now you're ready to hum back up to where you started. With each hum, slightly raise your pitch, while at the same time feeling the vibration of the sound moving from the base of your spine upward.
- When you have reached the highest pitch that you can comfortably make and the vibrations have reached the top of your head, you have completed the exercise.
- Sit quietly with your eyes closed for five minutes or so, noticing any changes in your body—tuning in to anything that you may have experienced while doing this exercise.

- When you feel ready, open your eyes. Begin to ground yourself, bringing your awareness back to your surroundings. Perhaps you'll want to wiggle your fingers or your toes, as this can help you feel grounded, bringing you back in your body. Once you feel fully present (and not at all light-headed or woozy), you can get up.

⌒ Encoding Intention

This exercise brings together much of what we have learned thus far with the actual encoding of intention. Once you have successfully experienced the power of humming with intention, you may decide to incorporate a humming practice on a daily basis.

Sometimes you have so many possible intentions to choose from that it becomes difficult to narrow it down to one single concept. If this is the case, remember that this exercise is only a beginning, and that tomorrow you can work on another aspect of intention. Simply choose one to start. This is, after all, an opportunity for you to experiment, remembering that you are your own best laboratory. A suggestion: one intention that is particularly easy to start with is appreciation; just imagine that you're projecting appreciation throughout your body as you're humming.

For this exercise, we suggest that you allow fifteen minutes—five minutes for humming, five minutes for relaxation, and five minutes for grounding. Please limit your actual humming to about five minutes.

- Close your eyes and take a few slow, deep diaphragmatic breaths, releasing any stress or tension in your body. As you're breathing in this manner, check yourself out—tune in and sense how you're feeling.
- Now spend a few moments contemplating what your intention will be. Spend as much time as you need determining how you would like to use your intention while humming.
- When you feel ready, begin to hum, remembering to make sure that you feel comfortable and that you're not straining your voice in any way. Hum knowing that you have a purpose—your intention has been set. You are engaged in conscious humming. Sometimes changing your pitch as you

project your hum is immensely helpful in being able to feel the resonance encoded with your intention.

- Hum for about five minutes. When you feel ready, bring your humming to a close.
- Sit quietly with your eyes closed for five minutes or so, noticing any changes in your body—tuning in to anything that you may have experienced while doing this exercise.
- When you feel ready, open your eyes. Begin to ground yourself, bringing your awareness back to your surroundings. Perhaps you'd like to wiggle your toes or your fingers, as this can help ground you, assisting in feeling yourself back in your body. Once you feel fully present (and not at all light-headed or woozy), you can get up.

When you first combine humming with intention, often the experience is quite profound. Can you feel a difference in your physical, emotional, or mental state after doing this exercise? Were you successful in encoding your intent onto your sound?

Processing Your Experience

If you achieved your desired effect with your intention and humming, we congratulate you. At the same time, we encourage you to be gentle with yourself and give yourself time to process your experience. How did you feel before you made the sound? Did you notice a difference in your physical, emotional, or mental state after you made the sound? You may have been more affected by this exercise than you think. It's important to assess yourself and your experience.

It's also important not to become discouraged if you didn't notice any specific changes after you have completed this or any of the exercises in this book. Perhaps your expectations were a bit high in terms of what you wanted to achieve. Five minutes of conscious humming may not, for example, immediately eradicate a chronic condition. Sometimes conditions that have been with us for a long time can disappear immediately and sometimes they need more healing time. It's also possible that you did receive slight relief in your condition, but you are just not yet aware of it.

Remember, babies don't begin walking immediately. First they have to learn to crawl. Then to stand. Then to take a step or two without falling. For many children, the process of learning to successfully walk takes a while. Anytime we learn something new, it can take a while, and it's important to be as gentle as possible with ourselves throughout the learning process.

With regard to combining our hum with our intention, we need to be satisfied with baby steps at first. Do not be disappointed if the purpose of your hum is not immediately achieved. For some people, success comes with the first try. For others, it's just a matter of time. As with most things, practice makes perfect; the more you practice conscious humming, the more skilled you will become in achieving results.

And please note—if you seem not to have experienced any effects, don't worry. We are all unique vibratory beings and experience things differently and in our own time. The more you work with and experience the power of sound (and silence), the more changes will manifest, the more you will be aware of them, and the easier they will come.

Effects of Subtle Energy

Sound is considered to be in the category of "energy" medicine. Many times it is categorized, like acupuncture, light therapy, and therapeutic touch, as a healing modality that utilizes "subtle energy." This is an energy that often must be sensed rather than felt since it is so "subtle" that it's sometimes difficult to feel it. An example of subtle energy is the electromagnetic field that surrounds the body, often called the "aura" or "auric field." Many different energy healers work with aspects of this field in order to affect the physical body.

While acknowledgment of subtle energy has yet to be documented in peer-reviewed scientific journals, some of the healing modalities that work with it, such as acupuncture, have been long tested and proven effective. While Western scientists have yet to definitively prove why it works, it's obvious that in China and many other countries where acupuncture is accepted and widely utilized, it would not have continued to be used for so many thousands of years if it did not work.

Probably the easiest explanation for how many of these subtle-energy healing modalities work is quite simple. As we noted earlier, everything is vibration, including our body. Thus, as also noted, an imbalance in the physical body is usually the result of a blockage of the energetic vibrations of the body—the natural harmonic resonance of the body, if you like. All that's necessary to remove the blockage is to change this out-of-tune vibration. Depending upon the condition and how long it has existed, changing the vibration and removing the blockage can be quite difficult or very easy.

How do we change blocked energy? It could be as uncomplicated as humming with intention to a particular area that has blocked energy. Think of it like a sonic massage. Have you ever had a kink in your arm (or another part of your body) that was quite painful? Most of us have. Then you massaged it a bit and suddenly the pain went away. What happened? On one level you could say that you had blocked energy that you loosened and then released as you massaged the painful spot. This is basically the same principle underlying the use of the hum.

You might ask how humming could possibly relieve a pain in, for example, your thigh. Once again, we bring your attention to the fact that through the use of sound as a subtle healing energy, it has the ability (with the help of your intent) to pass through your body to the place where you wanted it to vibrate and release the stuck energy.

This is definitely an intermediate to advanced level of working with sound, but we feel that at this point, having worked through all the preceding exercises, you are ready to take this on. When you sound your hum, we now encourage you to amplify your intention with a strong sense of belief. Rather than "thinking" that your hum may have a positive effect, *know* that your hum will have this effect, and feel it happening as you create the sound. This is a powerful way to use your imagination, and yet it is so very important in terms of enhancing your ability to project intention onto your sound.

7

The Yoga of Humming

Advanced Humming Practices

It seems like there are as many yoga studios these days as there are gyms and fitness centers. Yoga today is perhaps even more popular than aerobics was ten years ago. In fact, the two disciplines—yoga and aerobics—often are regarded by the layperson as being similar in terms of physical fitness.

We are both yoga enthusiasts, and have been for many years, and we know that yoga encompasses much more than the physical aspect of our well-being. In our current Western culture, yoga most commonly involves gathering a group of people and teaching them *asanas*, or postures, as part of the hatha yoga tradition. These postures are said to promote physical fitness, mobility, and other benefits. And this is true. However, the word *yoga* is actually a Sanskrit term that means "yoke" or "union," and the practice of yoga is a means by which we can support our body, our mind, and our spirit and come into alignment with the Divine. As we shall see, there are many yogic paths beside hatha yoga.

A recent search for different schools of yoga proved to be quite interesting. While the actual practice of legitimate yoga goes back thousands of years in India and incorporates many different practices, we found that there are only about a half dozen schools of yoga that are recognized in the West—all of which are variants of the hatha yoga tradition which focuses primarily on the body. In addition, most of these schools appear to have been established within the last twenty years or so. This phenomenon of the seeming newness of yoga in the West is most interesting to observe.

Different Paths of Yoga

As noted, yoga is quite ancient. There are numerous different schools, styles, and paths in yoga besides hatha. Here are but a few:

Bhakti yoga. This is devotional yoga and deals with meditation on the different gods and goddesses in the Hindu pantheon.

Karma yoga. This yoga consists of individuals being of entirely selfless service to the Divine through their actions in this life.

Laya yoga. This yoga, also known as kundalini yoga, focuses on the energy found within the spine and, in particular, in the chakras. It includes meditation, pranayama (breath work), and mantra yoga.

Mantra yoga. This yoga uses the repetition of sacred sounds for the practitioner to invoke and unite with specific energies and deities. The sacred sounds may be chanted vocally or repeated silently.

Raja yoga. This yoga seems to include all yogic styles and practices and focuses on mental mastery and meditation.

Shabd yoga. This yoga, also called called nada yoga, is the yoga of listening. Through listening, the practitioner can achieve deep states of meditation and union with the Divine.

Yantra yoga. This yoga focuses on the use of vision and form in order to create union with the Divine. Visualization is a primary facet of this practice.

As you can see, at least two yogic traditions—mantra yoga and shabd yoga—specifically involve sound. In addition, the use of sound is included in many other yogic traditions, such as devotional chanting in bhakti yoga and chakra chanting in laya yoga.

Humming and the Yoga Sutras

While we have utilized humming for many years, our interest in humming has been further reawakened through our yoga practice. We were teaching at Yogaville, the ashram founded by Sri Swami Satchidananda (he was the guru who led half a million people in chanting at the opening of the Woodstock Festival in 1969). While at Yogaville, we came across a copy of *The Yoga Sutras of Patanjali*, as translated by Sri Swami Satchidananda. Originally written around 400 CE, this book is one of the most well-known texts in any of the yogic traditions. We came across a verse, sutra 1.27. Here, Sri Swami Satchidananda explains that the original, fundamental sound of creation was the humming of *prana* (vital energy)—the sound of energy vibrating. This sound, later titled Ishwara, was given the name *Om*. Sri Swami Satchidananda writes:

> The word expressive of Isvara is the mystic sound Om. Because it is difficult to understand anything without a name, Patanjali wants to give the supreme *Purusha* a name. Even if He doesn't have a particular form, He should have a name. But "Isvara" is a limited name; "God" is also limited because the very vibrations of the letters are limited. So Patanjali wants a name that can give an unlimited idea and vibration and which can include all vibrations, all sounds and syllables, because God is like that—infinite. So Patanjali says His name is "Mmmm." We can't easily say "Mmmm," so it is written as Om. Om is called *pranava*, which simply means humming.*

We both did a double take as we realized that this esteemed spiritual master had stated that the sound at the beginning of all manifestation was the hum. This sound was then named *Om*.

Shortly after, we came upon an article by Reverend Jaganath Carrera

---

*Sri Swami Satchidananda, trans., *The Yoga Sutras of Patanjali* (Yogaville, Va.: Integral Yoga Publications, 1990), 42.

in *Integral Yoga* magazine in which he wrote about this same sutra:

> Sutra 1.27 The expression of Isvara is the mystic sound Om. This sutra introduces us to the name Om, which denotes Isvara. In Sanskrit, the word "Om" isn't mentioned. Instead, we find the term, pranava, the humming of prana. . . . Since pranava is not something we can easily chant, the name is given as Om. It is always vibrating within us, replaying the drama of creation, evolution and dissolution on many levels. This hum can be heard in deep meditation, when external sound is transcended and internal chatter stilled.*

Many years before this, Jonathan had created an award-winning album called *Ultimate Om* in which he recorded the sound *Om* being intoned by thousands of people in a temple, breathing at different times so that their voices overlapped. A few years later, Jonathan wondered what a recording of thousands of people humming (rather than chanting *Om*) would sound like. Would there be a difference? He created a new album titled *Cosmic Hum*. And indeed, there were great similarities in the sounds of the two recordings. This experimentation revived for both of us an interest in the power of the hum. Next came our journey into validation of its power.

After we had returned from teaching at Sri Swami Satchidananda's ashram, we contacted an expert in the yogic traditions (who happened to be our neighbor at the time) and asked him about the relationship between humming and yoga. He sent us an e-mail with two words: "bhramari pranayama."

Investigating Bhramari Pranayama

We knew that pranayama is the science of breath in the yogic traditions. A little investigation revealed that the term *bhramari pranayama*

---

*Reverend Jaganath Carrera, "Inside the Yoga Sutras: The Mystic OM," *Integral Yoga Magazine* (Winter 2009).

is Sanskrit for "humming bee breath," and it is, at a basic level, a practice of the self-created sounds of humming.

As we researched bhramari pranayama, we learned that it was said to have many physiological benefits—benefits that were very similar to those that are attributed to humming, as we described in chapter 1. The benefits listed below are a compilation of information that we found on various websites that focused on bhramari pranayama.*

In particular, bhramari pranayama is said to:

- Invigorate the thyroid gland, boosting metabolism
- Balance hormonal secretions
- Trigger serotonin release, resulting in balanced moods
- Help balance blood sugar levels
- Enhance the oxidization of fats in the body
- Be helpful for Alzheimer's disease
- Improve hearing[†]
- Help relieve migraines
- Produce quick and lasting relaxation
- Support the cardiovascular system
- Release heat from the body through perspiration and help you feel rejuvenated
- Help regulate blood circulation and lower blood pressure
- Help control respiratory disorders, asthma, and thyroid problems
- Regulate the endocrine system to support a healthy pregnancy and facilitate an easy childbirth
- Help build confidence
- Improve the functioning of the nervous system
- Activate the pituitary gland
- Improve concentration, memory, and alertness

---

*These included: www.yogicwayof life.com, www.artofliving.org, www.quora.com, www .theayurveda.org, www.sarvyyoga.com, and www.yogawiz.com.
†Mahendra Kumar Taneja, "Nitric Oxide Bhramari Pranayam and Deafness," *Indian Journal of Otology* 22, no. 1 (2016).

- Awaken kundalini energy
- Help treat paralysis
- Relieve sinus infections
- Stimulate the pineal gland
- Cure insomnia
- Charge and energize the central nervous system and the cortex of the brain
- Give the practitioner a good sonorous voice
- Relieve throat ailments
- Relieve the mind of anger, agitation, frustration, and anxiety

That's a lot of benefits! You might think that it's not possible for a simple practice of self-created sound to have such astonishing healing power. While it's true that many of these claims have not been scientifically validated, it is most interesting that they are found in so many different and varying sources regarding the benefits of bhramari pranayama. Kundalini, for example, a potent life energy that resides in the spine and that figures prominently in many systems of energy medicine, cannot at present be measured by any known instrument. So when we say that bhramari pranayama awakens kundalini, we have no scientific documentation to back up that statement. This doesn't mean that kundalini is not real. Anyone who has had the experience of kundalini rising up his or her spine is aware of its power. It simply means we can't measure it—yet.

We have seen many extraordinary occurrences happen in our work with sound, including, of course, astonishing healings. But as Jonathan mentioned in his first book, *Healing Sounds,* the cameras and research teams are usually not there when the miracles are happening. This does not mean that the miracles did not occur. Nor does it mean that the thousands of people who have reported phenomenal healings from sound are not being truthful. We mention this because in our next chapter we are going to suggest some things that may seem incredible or unbelievable. This does not mean that they are not possible or not true.

Recently, we were watching an episode of *Nova* on television. This particular episode involved relationships between species—one was of a dog and a cheetah behaving like good friends, while another involved a goat that took it upon itself to help guide a blind horse back and forth to pasture. It was quite amazing and truly heartwarming to watch these animals interacting. One of the scientists narrating the program suggested that such relationships indicated some sort of empathy between animals and that these anecdotes required further study. Then he said something that seemed so relevant to our own work that we wrote it down. It was this: "The plural of anecdote is data." What he meant was, if enough people report a phenomenon (an anecdote), the odds are that it's probably true (it becomes data).

Om versus Hum

There are many sources that describe how to practice bhramari pranayama, but, of course, they all vary somewhat. This fits in well with our principle of maintaining fluidity in the humming practice; you hum in the manner that seems best suited to you, as a unique vibratory being. With bhramari pranayama, there seems to be, in particular, some debate over whether the sound being made is an *Om* or a hum. Here, for example, is one description of bhramari pranayama:

> In this breathing practice your lips are supposed to be shut, and you are supposed to gently and smoothly make a sound like a humming bee in your throat. This simple practice is very helpful in making the breath smooth and quieting the mind. You can feel the sound vibrations in your throat, jaws, and face. This practice is so simple and straightforward, it can be done by anyone, regardless of age or background.*

Another description comes from a phenomenal article from Nepal Medical College that we mentioned in chapter 1, titled "Immediate

---

*K. Pederson, "Bhramari Pranayama (Humming Bee Breath)," December 17, 2012, http://www.yogawiz.com/articles/83/yoga-breathing-pranayama/bhramari.html.

Effect of a Slow Pace Breathing Exercise Bhramari Pranayama on Blood Pressure and Heart Rate":

> During exhalation the subject must chant the word "O-U-Mmmm" with a humming nasal sound mimicking the sound of a humming wasp, so that the laryngeal walls and the inner walls of the nostril mildly vibrate.*

From our perspective, the sounds of *Om* and humming have the same effect in the body. As we discussed in chapter 5, the sound *Om* can be seen as a precursor to humming. We have seen that some people have difficulty making a strictly humming sound. But if they add a brief "oh" to start their hum, they can then easily close their mouth and find that they are creating a powerful "mmmm" hum. And, of course, given the discourse from Swami Satchidananda (see pages 82, 83), the two sounds are intimately related.

Mudras

Bhramari pranayama is a breathing practice in which you gently and smoothly hum. Since we've been doing this for all the exercises in this book, you could say that you have already been practicing bhramari pranayama.

Some forms of bhramari pranayama also call for the use of mudras. Mudras are hand positions that have sacred as well as energetic significance. Incorporating mudras seems to be a more authentic and advanced form of this yogic technique. The simplest of the mudras used for bhramari pranayama calls for gently pressing two of your fingers on the cartilage over each ear to gently block the ears (see fig. 7.1 on page 88). It has the same effect as if you were to place your palms over your ears to block out sound.

---

*T. Pramanik, B. Pudasaini, and R. Prajapati, *Nepal Medical College Journal* 12, no. 3 (September 2010): 154–57.

Before we had ever heard of bhramari pranayama, we had tried blocking our ears while humming. It seemed to make our humming much louder while quieting all other external sounds. Because of this, it focused both our sound (our voice) and our capacity to listen. Ultimately, it made the experience more profound and powerful, enhancing the meditational experience that accompanies this practice.

There are more complex mudras that are said to enhance the effects of bhramari pranayama even more (see fig. 7.2). According to most teachings of this yogic practice, the inclusion of *shanmukhi* mudra is a more advanced way of performing bhramari pranayama. One variation of this mudra is performed as follows: Raise your arms up with the

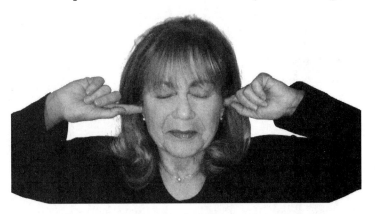

Fig. 7.1. A simple mudra for bhramari pranayama:
gently blocking each ear by pressing on the cartilage at the ear opening

Fig. 7.2. A variation of the shanmukhi mudra:
the more advanced mudra for bhramari pranayama

elbows out and block your ears by placing the tips of your thumbs over the ears. Do not apply any pressure. Now place your index fingers on the side of your head. The next three fingers should be placed over your forehead so that the little finger is just above your closed eyes.*

We personally did not find any significant difference between the gentle blocking of the ears accomplished in the simple mudra and the blocking of the more advanced mudra. We suggest that you try both mudras in order to experience each of them for yourself. Please note that as we investigated bhramari pranayama, we found inconsistencies and contradictions in the information we uncovered about this yogic practice. Some sources said that all the breathing needed to be through your nose. Others said that the first breath should be through the mouth and the next breath through the nose. Some sources said the hum should be of high pitch, while others said that a low pitch is recommended.

Since we are great advocates of fluidity—especially when working with sound—we were not bothered by the many varieties of breath, sound, and mudras associated with bhramari pranayama. From our perspective, as long as you've blocked your ears and are humming comfortably, you are undoubtedly practicing some form of this yogic technique.

However, we'd like to acknowledge that bhramari pranayama is an advanced yogic technique, and it is most important to remember that the purpose of yogic practices is to unite with higher aspects of consciousness. The practice of bhramari pranayama is sacred and potent and should be regarded as such. It is, of course, an extraordinary example of the conscious use of the hum.

Mindfulness

We have not yet spoken of mindfulness, and it's mandatory that we do—especially since mindfulness is becoming more and more of a

---

*https://yogainternational.com/article/view/5-ways-to-practice-bhramari (accessed February 15, 2017).

buzzword as a term for a deep form of meditation that puts you in the "now." Jon Kabat-Zinn, the founder of the mindfulness-based stress reduction technique, is perhaps the best-known proponent of this subject in the West, and so we give you his definition of mindfulness: "paying attention, on purpose, in the present moment, nonjudgmentally, to the unfolding of experience moment to moment."*

Mindfulness seems to naturally occur through our intentionalized experiences with humming. We believe that when you have completed your humming exercises, and you are checking yourself out and being present in the moment, you are indeed practicing mindfulness.

Mindfulness, like meditation, has many purposes. One of them, of course, is the reduction of stress. Another is connection to higher levels of consciousness. We know that during the humming exercises that we have recommended, you will have actually begun to experience both of these attributes.

⌒ Bhramari Pranayama

Now let's prepare to experience bhramari pranayama. In order to differentiate it from the other exercises in this book, we thought it would be excellent to include the use of one of the two mudras that have just been shown. Look back at the figures and descriptions (see pages 87, 88, 89) and decide which one you would like to use.

There are many ways to experience bhramari pranayama. You can simply listen to the sound of your humming, or you can focus your awareness on feeling the vibrations in your body. You can even use your imagination to travel on the humming sound to higher levels of consciousness. In the yogic tradition of sound, listening to the inner sounds that may be heard while you are humming (or afterward as you are sitting in silence) is considered to be among the most profound and powerful meditation practices, and it can be an extraordinary way to unite with the Divine. This approach to working with bhramari pranayama is perhaps the most advanced of the many variations that exist.

---

*www.mindful.org/jon-kabat-zinn-defining-mindfulness (accessed February 9, 2017).

For this exercise we suggest that you allow fifteen minutes—five minutes for humming, five minutes for relaxation, and five minutes for grounding. Please limit your actual humming to about five minutes.

- Close your eyes and take a few slow, deep diaphragmatic breaths, releasing any stress or tension in your body. As you're breathing in this manner, check yourself out—tune in and sense how you're feeling.
- Decide upon one of the previously described mudras and place your hands in the position of the mudra you plan to use.
- When you feel ready, begin to hum, remembering to make sure that you feel comfortable and that you're not straining your voice in any way. Listen to your hum, feel its resonance, encode it with your intention to unite with the Divine, or whatever method feels right to you.
- Hum for about five minutes. When you feel ready, bring your humming to a close.
- Bring your hands down to your lap and relax. Now sit quietly for five minutes or so, and in that state of silence, tune in to what you are experiencing in this present moment. Allow yourself sufficient time to enjoy this space of relaxation and peace.
- When you feel ready, open your eyes. Begin to ground yourself, bringing your awareness back to your surroundings. Perhaps you'll want to wiggle your toes or your fingers, as this can help you feel yourself back in your body. Once you feel fully present (and not at all light-headed or woozy), you can get up.

Take a moment and feel a sense of appreciation for the experience you have just had. You may find the bhramari pranayama technique has made the experience of humming even more powerful. We trust you have enjoyed it.

8

The Humming Hypothesis

This chapter, the culmination of our work with humming, may contain the most important and significant material in this book. In truth, we wanted to create an uncomplicated book on the subject of humming, and we hope that so far it has been relatively easy to understand and user-friendly. However, as we delved more and more into the subject of this seemingly simplest of sounds, we discovered insights, connections, and far-reaching possibilities that superseded our desire to write a simple book on humming. In this chapter, we'll go into these more complex investigations. For some, this may be the best part.

We began this book with information on the power of self-created sound—specifically humming—that came from peer-reviewed scientific research, articles, and papers. As this book progressed, we began adding more and more topics that are not particularly conventional but that we felt were relevant, such as the concept of intent, heart-brain coherence, and quantum fields of possibilities. Now, it is our pleasure to conclude this book by speculating on some extremely powerful, though currently unproven, potential phenomena of humming. This—the vast, untapped transformational potential underlying humming—is our forward-looking humming hypothesis.

What Is a Hypothesis?

The Merriam-Webster dictionary succinctly defines a hypothesis as this: "an idea or theory that is not proven but that leads to further study or discussion."* And indeed, we have found that from a scientific perspective, research has provided evidence and data for our humming hypothesis, but further study and discussion are needed.

As was suggested by the scientist we mentioned in our last chapter, a series of anecdotes is data. On one level, this was meant as a joke. On another level, he was being quite serious. When a phenomenon is reported again and again, eventually it comes to be seen as true. Just because a phenomenon has not yet been proven by clinical research or scientific measurement does not mean it is not true; it just means it has not yet been proven. It is still in the anecdotal stage. Its time will come. Thus, while some aspects of our humming hypothesis have yet to be proven, much of it is based upon scientifically validated physiological phenomena. We share it with you because we believe it is true.

Neurons and Neural Networks

A neuron, or nerve cell, is an electrically excitable cell in our brain that processes and transmits information by electrical and chemical signaling. Neurons communicate with each other by sending impulses (electrochemical signals) across the small gaps, or synapses, between them. Neurons connect to each other to form neural networks. Each neuron has three basic parts:

1. Cell body or soma. This main part has all the key components of the cell, including the nucleus, chromosomes, endoplasmic reticulum, ribosomes, and mitochondria.

---

*As defined on Merriam-Webster.com, January 17, 2017, https://www.merriam-webster .com/dictionary/hypothesis.

2. Axon. This lengthy, cable-like projection carries electrochemical impulses along the length of the cell. The axon is often covered by a myelin sheath.

3. Dendrites. These branch-like projections of the cell receive signals from other neurons, allowing the cells to communicate with each other.

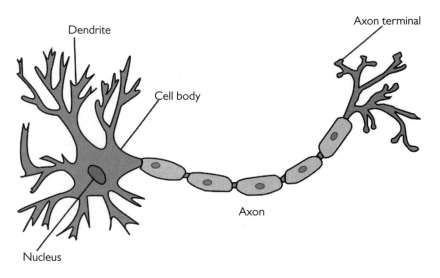

Fig. 8.1. A neuron showing the cell body, axon, and dendrites

Many years ago, when Jonathan was engaged in a Ph.D. program at Union Institute and University, he studied the psychophysiology of sound—that is, how sound affects the physical, emotional, and mental aspects of a human being. His hypothesis at the time was that, just as electrical impulses are able to stimulate neurons, it could be possible to use the vibrations of self-created sound to stimulate neurons in order to create new neural networks and potentially regenerate damaged neurons (see fig. 8.2).

Such a phenomenon would have great potential for repairing injured brain tissue, with significant implications for the treatment of Alzheimer's disease, strokes, head injuries, and more. Today, the study of neurogenesis confirms that it is indeed possible to grow new neurons.

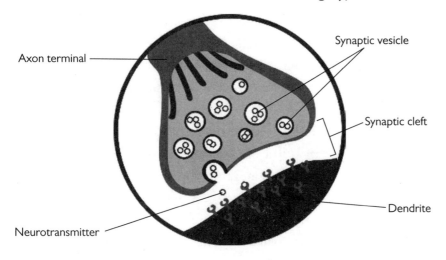

Axon terminal

Synaptic vesicle

Synaptic cleft

Dendrite

Neurotransmitter

Fig. 8.2. The neural synapse between axon and dendrite

The study of the relationship between sound and neurogenesis is ongoing, with several interesting twists.

Microtubule Vibrations

In the early 1990s, at the Sound Colloquium, a conference for sound healers and therapists in Epping, New Hampshire, Susan Gallagher Borg, a renowned sound therapist, spoke with Jonathan about the concept of microtubules and their connection with the healing power of sound. Microtubules are fibrous, tube-shaped protein structures that help support and shape cells. However, at the time, little was known about them.

Years later, in 2014, we were sent material about a recent discovery of quantum vibrations in microtubules inside the brain. As it turns out, microtubules vibrate at incredible frequencies—ten million vibrations per second. Their vibrations are thought to be responsible for brainwave activity, and as the study authors conclude:

Treating brain microtubule vibrations could benefit a host of mental, neurological, and cognitive conditions. . . . Clinical trials of brief brain stimulation aimed at microtubule resonances with megahertz mechanical vibrations using transcranial ultrasound have shown reported improvements in mood, and may prove useful against Alzheimer's disease and brain injury in the future.*

Scientists have focused much of their work in using sound to affect brain cells in the ultrasound range, which, perhaps not coincidentally, vibrates in the same megahertz frequencies as microtubules. It could be that the reason scientists are finding ultrasound to be an effective tool for neurological treatments is that it synchronizes with microtubule vibrations, which could themselves possibly be the source of or contribute to brain waves. But self-created sounds like humming don't even begin to approach the incredible high frequencies of ultrasound. Is it even possible for humming to affect brain waves? We speculate that the answer is yes, based on a phenomenon known as "beat frequencies." It has been suggested by Stuart Hameroff, M.D., and Sir Roger Penrose, authors of an article titled "Consciousness in the Universe: A Review of the 'Orch OR' Theory,"† that the microtubule vibrations interact with each other and create much slower frequencies which fall within the audible range and are called beat frequencies.

Beat Frequencies

According to the physics of sound, beat frequencies occur whenever two slightly different frequencies resonate together. When these two frequencies sound, they create a third frequency, which is the vibrational difference between the first two frequencies. As an example, a frequency of 100 Hz and a frequency of 110 Hz together create a third

---

*"Discovery of Quantum Vibrations in 'Microtubules' Corroborates Theory of Consciousness," Phys.org, January 16, 2014, https://phys.org/news/2014-01-discovery-quantum-vibrations-microtubules-corroborates.html.
†*Physics of Life Reviews* 11, no. 1 (2014): 39–78.

frequency, which is the difference between them—that is, 10 Hz, which is called the "difference tone."

If one frequency is directed into one ear, and another slightly different frequency is directed into the opposite ear, as might happen if you were wearing headphones, the resulting difference tone would also be known as the "binaural beat frequency." The term *binaural* refers to the process of directing independent sounds separately to the two ears of the listener. Research indicates that binaural beat frequencies can synchronize and balance the predominant lobes of the left and right hemispheres of the brain. Perhaps most importantly, when the binaural beat frequencies are between 1 and 25 Hz, they have the ability to actually entrain with our brain waves. In other words, our brain waves resonate with these frequencies. This is true whether the two source frequencies are vibrating in a low range (like our example of 100 Hz and 110 Hz producing a difference tone of 10 Hz) or in a very high range, in the thousands of thousands of cycles per second or greater. The important factor is that the difference between them—the beat frequency—lies within the frequency range of our brain waves. In our next section, you will see that brain waves can operate at frequencies of up to 100 Hz. However, research of binaural beat frequencies to entrain the brain has been primarily limited to the brain-wave ranges of 1 to 25 Hz.*

Brain Waves

Our brain waves pulsate and oscillate at particular frequencies that can be measured in cycles per second, just like sound waves. There are four basic delineations of different brain-wave states:

Beta waves—from 14 to 25 Hz. Beta waves occur in our normal waking state of consciousness. Beta waves are present when our focus of attention is on activities of the external world.

---

*Jonathan Goldman, "Sonic Entrainment," in *Music Medicine,* ed. Ralph Spintge, M.D. and Roland Droh, M.D., 194–208 (St. Louis, Mo.: MMB Music Inc., 1992).

Alpha waves—from 8 to 13 Hz. Alpha waves occur when we daydream and are often associated with a state of meditation. Alpha waves become stronger and more regular when our eyes are closed.

Theta waves—from 4 to 7 Hz. Theta waves are found in states of high creativity and have been equated to the states of consciousness associated with shamanic work. Theta waves also occur in states of deep meditation and sleep.

Delta waves—from 0.5 to 3 Hz. Delta waves occur in states of deep sleep or unconsciousness. In addition, modern brain-wave research indicates that a state of deep meditation can produce delta waves in conscious individuals.

In addition, there is another frequency range that has recently come into study:

Gamma waves—approximately 25 to 100 Hz. These higher-frequency brain waves have been found in seasoned meditators and are often associated with profound insight and deep integration of ideas or experiences.

As you can see, most of the frequencies produced by brain waves are within the lower range of audible sound. Some are below this range. Earlier in this book we discussed how harmonics within the audible range have the ability to affect both infrasound and ultrasound. We suggested that the harmonics of the human voice could resonate with our brain waves and that our brain waves could be entrained by our voice, in much the same way binaural beat frequencies can entrain the brain. Scientific evidence proves that this is true—that our self-created sounds can entrain portions of our brain and that these sounds can be beneficial for many different purposes, including stress reduction and clarity of thought.[*]

---

[*]Jonathan Goldman, "Sonic Entrainment," in *Music Medicine,* ed. Ralph Spintge, M.D. and Roland Droh, M.D.

Neuroplasticity

Another interesting aspect of brain activity that has great importance with regard to our humming hypothesis is the concept of neuroplasticity. Neuroscientist Paul King writes on the subject:

> Structural plasticity occurs when neurons grow new axons and synapses, altering the structure of the neural network. The axons tunnel their way through neural tissue, like roots growing in soil, until they bump into other neurons and form new synapses. Sometimes new wiring is added during brain development and then later removed (called "pruning").
>
> At a high level, neuroplasticity allows regions of the brain to reconfigure to serve new functions. For example, following a stroke, neuroplasticity allows surrounding brain tissue to take over from damaged regions.
>
> Every time a new memory is formed, the brain changes. If you can remember what you did yesterday, physical changes happened in the brain to store that memory, and that is neuroplasticity.*

Neuroplasticity is currently one of the more intriguing aspects of neurological research, with many scientists quite excited about the fact that the brain can remap itself after injury. We hypothesize that the vibrations of self-created sounds such as humming could stimulate neuroplasticity in the brain, allowing new neurons to generate and new synaptic connections to form.

Alzheimer's and Humming

The concepts of microtubule vibrations and neuroplasticity seem to point in the same direction with regard to the potential use of sound to affect the brain. In particular, sound healing may be of benefit in

---

*Paul King, answering the question "What is neuroplasticity and how does it work?" on Quora, updated August 21, 2013, http://www.quora.com/What-is-neuroplasticity-and -how-does-it-work.

cases of Alzheimer's. Research indicates that rhythmic sound—playing an instrument or singing—can improve clarity of mind in Alzheimer's patients, though the effect may not be long lasting. Other research indicates that such activities can induce relaxation, which seems to have positive benefits with regard to Alzheimer's.[*]

Recent research from March, 2015, has demonstrated that focused ultrasonic frequencies can gently open up the blood-brain barrier and stimulate microglial cells to clear toxic beta-amyloid plaques that sit between neurons and disrupt their transmissions. According to the report, in mice with Alzheimer's-like symptoms, ultrasound was able to restore memory in 75 percent of the subjects.[†] The article said that human trials were slated to start in 2016.

We find the use of ultrasound as a potential treatment of Alzheimer's to be extremely encouraging. Currently, there is no known healing modality that will alleviate or cure this condition. While the use of ultrasound is only in the beginning stages of research, this treatment represents a nonpharmacological and noninvasive approach to Altzheimer's. The results are very promising. In addition, as previously noted, due to beat frequencies and other phenomenon of sound such as harmonics, it may be possible to resonate portions of the brain and achieve similar results to those achieved with ultrasound using self-created audible sounds such as humming.[‡] This hypothesis may be a reason why one of the reported benefits of bhramari humming is that it is "helpful for Alzheimer's disease."[§] Another article on bhramari pranayama discusses the importance of nitric oxide generated through this yogic technique and states: "It potentiates immunity and senile

---

[*]www.mayoclinic.org/diseases-conditions/alzheimers-disease/expert-answers/music-and-alzheimers/FAQ-20058173

[†]Gerhard Leinenga and Jürgen Götz, "Scanning ultrasound removes amyloid-β and restores memory in an Alzheimer's disease mouse model," *Science Translational Medicine* 7, no. 278 (2015): 278ra33.

[‡]For more on the potential of sound healing, see Jonathan's book *Healing Sounds: The Power of Harmonics* (Healing Arts Press, 2002).

[§]www.yogawiz.com

degeneration (dementia Alzheimer's)."* It seems as if this ancient humming practice may have been observed to have positive effects on those suffering from Alzheimer's and other similar imbalances.

Brain Trauma and Humming

Could humming—particularly humming with intent—positively affect traumatic conditions of the brain? If humming has the ability to generate, restore, and rejuvenate neurons in the brain, as our hypothesis posits, this concept appears quite plausible.

Unfortunately, we have only anecdotal information with regard to our hypothesis. However, we can relate numerous stories of people to whom we've suggested the use of humming after a head trauma and from whom we later received corroboration of positive results.

Stroke and Humming

We don't usually talk in detail about specific cases because it seems like an invasion of privacy. But here we make an exception because the patient is a member of our family and gave us permission. Andi's mother had a stroke—a vascular stroke. Initially she did not seem to have any noticeable aftereffects, but within a day or two after the stroke, we both began to become aware of a slight slurring in her speech. In fact, though she remained coherent, the slurring seemed to get progressively worse, hour by hour, as we talked to her. We were concerned.

We asked her if she would do us a favor. We asked her if she would find out from her doctor in which part of her brain the stroke had occurred and then hum for just five minutes, imagining the sound of the hum going into that area, stimulating the part of her brain that needed help.

Andi's mother is a wonderful person who at the time was in her late eighties. She knew of our out-of-the-ordinary activities working with sound and was therefore not too shocked when we asked her to do this. We

---

*M. K. Taneja, "Bhramari (Shanmukhi Mudra) Pranayama in presbyacusis and dementia," *Indian Journal of Otology* 22 (2016): 145–47.

thought there was a good possibility that she would start humming for us. We did not, however, mention our awareness of a change in her speech, nor did we talk to her doctor. We thought her doctor might think this woman's family needed hospitalization themselves if they thought that humming might do anything to assist her condition. And besides, whether or not the doctor thought the humming "treatment" had any possible validity, it all depended upon Andi's mother. It was she who had to do the humming.

We called her the next day and there seemed to be a slight and positive change in her speech, but it was difficult to tell. The following day, we really thought something was going on. Her voice was clearer and we could understand her better. By the third day, her speech was back to normal.

We are aware that Andi's mother might well have recovered her normal speech without humming, as a part of the normal recovery process. We are also aware that this story is anecdotal. But we have many more stories like it of people using humming to assist with stroke and neurological disorders. We cannot help but repeat to you the concept that the plural of anecdote is data.

For those of you with family or friends who are suffering from stroke, Alzheimer's, or brain trauma, we highly suggest that you do your best to encourage them to try humming, as we did with Andi's mom. Check in with the medical staff, making sure they approve of this practice, but the odds are that they won't have any difficulty. Our experience is that most medical practitioners don't take the subject of humming seriously. Perhaps this book may help change their minds.

PTSD and Humming

One of our great hopes has been to introduce the power of humming to veterans with post-traumatic stress disorder (PTSD). Some research has indicated that listening to soothing music can help in reducing stress with those suffering from this disorder.* Dr. George Lindenfeld,

---

*M. Bensimon, E. Bodner, and A. Shrira, "The emotional impact of national music on young and older adults differing in posttraumatic stress disorder symptoms," *Aging & Mental Health* (June 2016): 1–9 [Epub ahead of print].

a neuropsychologist and the author of several books on PTSD, including *Brain on Fire: A Therapist's Guide to Extinguishing the Flames of PTSD*, has developed a procedure that uses binaural beat frequencies to successfully treat veterans with PTSD. In addition, when the specific instrumentation utilized to apply binaural beat frequencies to his clients was not available, Dr. Lindenfeld suggested that his clients hum at specific frequencies.

Currently, there has not been adequate research on the use of binaural beat frequencies or self-created sound to treat PTSD to convince doctors and counselors to include these therapies in their treatment protocols. However, we trust this will change.

We have worked with a number of veterans who have suffered from PTSD and have utilized humming as a means of helping alleviate their symptoms. One participant, named Tony (name changed to create anonymity), has written to us, asking that his experience be shared with others:

"In general, when I practice meditation and humming with *Cosmic Hum,* I have noticed a significant decrease in my irritability, anger, disassociation with the present moment and nightmares. The decrease in nightmares is a welcome change as I have had nightmares and night terrors with audible screaming and thrashing for about thirty years. I do NOT have the same level of tranquility, clarity and rest when I neglect my humming practices and just leave it up to the meds."[*]

Tony has now begun facilitating programs with other veterans suffering from PTSD on his own, using materials we have given him on humming. We are hopeful that sometime soon, humming will become a significant part of the regimen for treating PTSD.

We have created a brief manual, *Humming for Health,* that we have made available for both clients and therapists working with PTSD. It is available for downloading from our website at www.healingsounds.com/HummingForHealth.

---

[*]Personal communication to Jonathan and Andi Goldman, August 26, 2015.

Concluding Thoughts

From both peer-reviewed research and our own experiences, we know that humming creates an almost immediate calming effect and is a supportive treatment for stress. There's no doubt about it—we ourselves use humming whenever we feel ourselves getting tense, and then we feel better.

It appears, however, that much of the medical community at this time prefers to treat stress with pharmaceuticals. Certain colleagues of ours in the medical arena have had success using humming with their patients, but the majority of MDs to whom we've suggested humming as a therapeutic practice seem skeptical and uninterested in pursuing the potential benefits. We've run into a lot of red tape with regard to implementing humming in medical settings. This does not mean that humming doesn't work; it simply means that it has not yet reached mainstream acceptance. We continue to work, teach, and investigate, and we look forward to the time in the future when humming will be used to its maximum potential.

What is that maximum potential? Let's restate our humming hypothesis. The theory is this: The act of humming creates vibrations within the brain that stimulate a plethora of neurochemicals, such as melatonin and nitric oxide, as well as microtubules of different cells in the brain. The vibrational effect stimulates the repair of damaged or diseased cells, the generation of new cells, and the formation of new synaptic pathways. Simply put: it is possible to create new neural networks in the brain through self-created sound such as humming. This is the humming hypothesis, and we believe it has great implications with regard to Alzheimer's, strokes, various head injuries, PTSD, and many other conditions and diseases related to neurological imbalances, as well as an overall state of physical, emotional, and spiritual well-being. We trust that very soon the power of humming to create positive and beneficial vibrational effects will become recognized and validated by the scientific and medical communities and used to assist the healing process.

A New Beginning

We now come to the end of this book. At this point in your reading, you will have begun to realize the incredible potential of humming, including the extraordinary possibility that the hum may well have been the original sound of creation. Thus, it feels most appropriate to suggest that here, rather than reaching an ending, you have entered into "A New Beginning."

We trust that this book will help guide you along your journey with sound as a healing modality, with a special emphasis on the power of the hum and, in particular, the conscious hum. Perhaps it will give you a new awareness of the power of sound, particularly if you have never considered humming in any serious fashion.

There is so much fascinating material on the hum that we have not included in this book. But in our attempt to keep the information about humming as uncomplicated as possible, we decided that we could not present it all. We have, however, decided that we would be remiss if we did not include some mention of humming bees—particularly since we did devote a chapter to bhramari pranayama, and, as you may recall, the word *bhramari* is Sanskrit for "humming bee."

To begin, we sing (or should we say hum!) the praises of the humming bee. This small but magnificent creature pollinates flowers, makes honey, and fills the world with its buzzing, humming energy. Without the humming bee, life would be very different on this planet. In fact, there are many legends from different traditions about bee deities, such as the bee god in the Mayan tradition who is a transdimensional shifter of energy.

Doctorates in Bioenergetic Medicine and teachers of the ancient Egyptian healing and spiritual tradition, Meredith McCord and Jill Schumacher shared information with us about the Bee Teachings of ancient Egypt and the sounding practices associated with these teachings. In this ancient tradition, the humming sound of the bee was said to stimulate the release of super hormones known as the "Elixirs of Metamorphosis." This sound also resonates the ventricular chambers in the center of the brain, which are filled with cerebrospinal fluid. Cerebrospinal fluid (CSF) is a clear, colorless body fluid found in the brain and spine. Produced in the ventricles of the brain, it acts as a cushion for the brain's cortex, providing basic mechanical and immunological protection to the brain inside the skull. CSF also circulates nutrients and filters chemicals from the blood, removes waste products from the brain, and transports hormones to other areas of the brain. (Many different spiritual traditions also believe this fluid is sacred and is the conduit for vital life energy that travels up and down the spine and into the brain). Doctors McCord and Schumacher also told us that the humming sounds of the bee resonate and stimulate various structures of the brain, including the pineal gland, pituitary gland, hypothalamus, and amygdala, whose functions we have discussed in other portions of this book.

We initially thought material about the humming bee would be too much of a digression to include in this book, but then a program on PBS—a documentary chronicling the disappearance of humming bees—sparked our interest. This is not a new phenomenon but one that has gained more and more mainstream attention in recent years.

Bees, it seems, are disappearing—they have been literally dying for no apparent reason. Their colonies are dispersing and they are vanishing. No one knows why, but it is not uncommon for dozens of honeybees to come tumbling from the sky—dead! Scientists and beekeepers alike are trying to discover the reason why so many bee colonies are breaking down. This phenomenon has been given a name: colony collapse disorder. It occurs when the majority of worker bees in a colony disappear, leaving behind the queen bee and a few nurse bees to care for the remaining immature bees. The bee colony cannot survive under these conditions.

As we know, bees make honey. They are also Mother Nature's way of pollinating plants and allowing their continued reproduction. If the mystery of colony collapse disorder continues, not only will bees disappear, but much of the flowering flora of the world—fruits, flowers, vegetables, and all kinds of wild plants—will suffer.

The PBS special did not resolve the dilemma, although there was a lot of anecdotal evidence to suggest that there was a relationship between colony collapse disorder and pesticides. This problem was on our minds when we took a walk together at Walden Ponds, a wilderness preserve near our house in Colorado.

The Bee Lady

On this particular Sunday, toward the end of December 2014, we were walking quietly through Walden Ponds when we passed a man and woman. Usually we would have smiled, said hello, and continued on our way. People walking through nature preserves generally don't like to be disturbed. But on this day, for some reason, we stopped and started talking with this lovely couple. Neither of us can remember how our conversation began, but we talked for a while, and eventually one of them asked us, "What do you do?"

When people we don't know ask us about our work, normally we say something about composing music for meditation and relaxation. It's much easier and less complicated than getting into the details of sound healing and the various layers of this work, since most people are unfamiliar with it. But somehow, on this day, we not only began talking in depth about the use of sound for healing, we told this lovely couple that we were writing a book on the healing properties of humming.

They then began to tell us about a friend of theirs who lived in the mountains outside of Boulder. This woman apparently worked with bees in a healing capacity. They told us how to contact her, and we did. Her name is Dr. Valerie Solheim, and she is called the "Bee Lady."

Valerie is a Jungian psychologist and beekeeper who uses the humming sounds of bees as an integral part of her healing sessions with clients. We traded a copy of Jonathan's album *Cosmic Hum* for one of her Healing Bees CDs. Her CDs are recordings of a humming beehive during different seasons and different activities. Continuing on with the synchronicity that seemed to have followed humming and bees, it turns out that the person who recorded Dr. Solheim's CDs was Kimba Arem, a prominent sound therapist and dear friend of ours.

Valerie had much to say about the healing power of the sound of bees. She related many stories about the powerful healings her clients had experienced when they listened to the Healing Bees CDs. Most extraordinary for us, however, was Dr. Solheim's claim that she had played one of her CDs for a hive with colony collapse disorder, and as a result the imbalanced hive had come back to a state of normalcy.

According to Dr. Solheim, the restoration of hives with colony collapse disorder is made possible thanks to the same principles we have been utilizing with sound healing for many years: vibrational resonance and entrainment. The colonies that were suffering from collapse disorder were simply resonating out of their natural harmony. The humming of healthy bees was able to entrain the distressed colony and help it heal.

This is just an anecdote, of course. However, considering all the information about sound, humming, and healing that we've disclosed in this book, it certainly makes sense to us.

We have received many e-mails and letters from people who have experienced healing through listening to Jonathan's *Cosmic Hum* recording. We have little doubt that listening to the humming sound of healthy bees could indeed be healing for both people and bees. And if listening to the sounds of healthy bees can heal colony collapse disorder, perhaps it could assist in averting a natural disaster.

More to Come

Having written a number of books on sound healing, we find that after one of our books has been published, we receive feedback from readers that validates and verifies much of the material in our writing. For all we know, someone at this very moment is doing research showing how self-created sound can rejuvenate damaged brain cells and create new brain circuitry. In many of our workshops, we suggest to our participants that this research needs to be done. And perhaps unbeknownst to us it is being done at this very moment.

We invite you to contact us at **info@healingsounds.com** with any affirming stories about humming. And we also invite you to share the significant power of humming with others—particularly those who might benefit from some of the potential effects of this healing sound.

As we conclude this book, we'd like to thank you for accompanying us on this most unique and remarkable journey. It has been our great joy to share with you our information on the benefits of humming. May your journey with humming continue to resonate and bring you many beautiful blessings!

Please listen to track 6 of the instructional audio tracks.

Many texts on sound healing and sacred sound might end with an *Om*. Instead, we'll end with a hum. Thus, we begin again: mmmm.

Please listen to track 7 of the instructional audio tracks.

How to Use
The Humming Effect
Instructional Audio Tracks

The audio tracks that accompany this book are designed to assist you on your journey toward experiencing the transformational power of your own hum. Download at

audio.innertraditions.com/humeff

Throughout this book, whenever an audio track is appropriate, we make the suggestion to listen to it. As we note in our introduction to the audio tracks, we've found that sometimes hearing an example of a humming exercise is very helpful. Since the quality and range of our voice is different for each of us, we're not expecting you to try to duplicate the way we sound. We're just giving you examples of what these exercises could sound like.

When you are practicing the exercises in this book, we suggest that you find a place where you can make sound without being disturbed. We also suggest that you sit with your back straight and follow the instructions we give for each exercise. You'll probably find it helpful to listen to the recorded example first and then try the exercise. Our first track is an introduction, which we trust will make even clearer the purpose of these audio tracks. The next four tracks are self-explanatory. The track that follows is a conclusion, which we trust you will also find helpful in assisting as you experience the amazing power of the hum. We recommend that you go through these tracks in the same order in which you encounter them in the book. When you come upon a statement that asks you to listen to a specific track, we suggest that you do so then and not before. The last track, "Constant Hum," is a recording of many hundreds of people humming together. We've found that having a recording such as this playing in the background can sometimes assist and make it even more fun if you hum along with it.

When you are making your own sound, remember that it's important to stay in your comfort zone, not straining your vocal cords. *Louder is not better, and it's **not** necessary to make a loud sound in order to experience the healing power of your own voice.* Last, please enjoy yourself when you make these sounds. When we find ourselves humming, we naturally feel good. As you become more consciously aware of your hum, remember to enjoy the experience.

1. Introduction   (2:18)
2. Working with the Vowel Sounds   (5:29)
3. How to Hum, Part I   (4:39)
4. How to Hum, Part II   (4:32)
5. Humming Your Spine   (1:48)
6. Conclusion   (1:39)
7. The Constant Hum   (17:43)

Recommended Resources

To our knowledge, *The Humming Effect* is the first in-depth book to be published on the subject of humming. We therefore cannot recommend any other books on humming. There are, however, myriad books and recordings that are relevant to the field of sound as a healing and transformational modality. Here are our suggestions. Many of them contain at least some discussion of humming. We have also included some of the books on other topics that we've mentioned in this book that deal with various aspects of breath, belief, and consciousness. In addition, we have presented some recordings that the reader may find of interest.

Books

Sound and Music Books by Jonathan Goldman and Andi Goldman

Chakra Frequencies by Jonathan Goldman and Andi Goldman (Destiny Books, 2011). This book, winner of a Coalition of Visionary Resources (COVR) Visionary Award for Best Alternative Health Book, examines the science of sound healing for higher consciousness, stronger relationships, planetary oneness, and physical and emotional healing. It offers exercises with breath, tone, sacred vowel sounds, and the chanted *bija* mantras to activate and balance the chakras for greater health and harmony.

Other Sound and Music Books by Jonathan Goldman

The Divine Name (Hay House, 2016). This COVR Visionary Award winner is a step-by-step guide to vibratory activation. This book will allow you to experience the power, majesty, and healing of the Divine Name, a universal sound created from vowels that enhances resonance with the Divine. Also included are audio downloads of instructional material and a sacred sound invocation to help you learn to intone and more powerfully experience the Divine Name.

Healing Sounds (Healing Arts Press, 2002). Considered a classic in the field of sound healing, this book contains much material on the spiritual and scientific aspects of sound healing. In particular, it focuses upon the use of voice as a healing instrument and the subject of harmonics. Readers will find it filled with information and exercises that will enhance the power of sound as a healing modality.

The 7 Secrets of Sound Healing, revised edition (Hay House, 2017). These seven "secrets" are the basic principles of how sound can be used to heal and transform. Each chapter, dedicated to one of these principles, has clear and concise information based upon Jonathan's many years of working with sound. Topics include frequency, intent, silence, and vibrations. This book is a wonderful introduction and resource guide to the subject of sound healing.

Shifting Frequencies (Light Technology, 2010). Originally compiled from a column that Jonathan wrote for *Sedona Journal of Emergence* magazine, this book covers the gamut of both scientific and spiritual information about sound. It includes chapters on harmonics, breath, vocalization and visualization, mantras, God-name chanting, color and light, quartz crystals, and much more.

Sound and Music Books by Other Authors

Cymatics: A Study of Wave Phenomena and Vibration by Hans Jenny (Macromedia, 2001). An extraordinary book of breathtaking photographs by Swiss doctor Hans Jenny, demonstrating the ability of sound to create form. This is proof of the power of sound to affect physical matter.

The Ear and the Voice by Alfred Tomatis (Scarecrow, 2004). This book introduces the concepts of Dr. Tomatis as they apply to singing and how the ear functions in relation to the brain and the rest of the body. It also gives practical advice on singing, posture, and matters pertaining primarily to musicians.

The Effects of Sound on People by James P. Cowan (Wiley, 2016). This is a very up-to-date and scientific overview of how we hear and how sound affects us on a physical and emotional level. Much of it is dedicated to the negative aspects of sound—particularly noise pollution. There is a chapter on the positive effects of sound.

The Healing Forces of Music by Randall McClellan (iUniverse, 2000). Though published some years ago, the information in this book is still valid and relevant today. McClellan's book contains much valuable and important material on the history, theory, and practice of different systems that utilize sound and music for healing and transformation.

The Healing Power of the Human Voice by James D'Angelo (Healing Arts Press, 2005). D'Angelo examines the healing attributes of the human vocal expression, from vowels and consonants to the natural sounds of laughter and sighs, the power of singing, and classical chants and mantras from cultures around the world. He shows how we can create various vocal forms to contribute to our physical and mental health.

The Healing Power of Sound by Mitchell L. Gaynor (Shambhala, 2002). Dr. Gaynor presents his sound-based techniques for self-healing—techniques that anyone can use, whether faced with a life-threatening disease or simply seeking relief from the stresses of daily life. This text includes twelve exercises involving breathing, meditation, and toning that can be used by anyone to improve their health and quality of life.

Human Tuning by John Beaulieu (Biosonics, 2010). This groundbreaking work integrates science, sound, and spirituality in teaching readers how to tune their body with tuning forks. When we tune ourselves, we tune our nervous system, achieving greater balance, harmony, and wellness in our lives. It is truly one of the best books on sound healing.

The Mozart Effect by Don Campbell (Avon, 1997). One of the most important books for mainstream readers about music as medicine for the body, the mind, and the soul. Campbell shows how modern science has begun to confirm this ancient wisdom, finding evidence that listening to certain types of music can improve our quality of life in almost every respect.

Music and Sound in the Healing Arts by John Beaulieu (Station Hill, 1987). This small and extremely readable book contains much valuable information on the therapeutic and transformational uses of sound and music. It addresses mantras, tuning forks, voice energetics, and much more. Beaulieu has been a great teacher and friend of ours and we highly recommend his book.

The Mysticism of Sound and Music by Hazrat Inayat Khan (Shambhala, 1996). This is one of the most important books on the power of sound. Initially written in the early 1900s, the information is as fresh and valid today as it was when it first appeared. Topics include the effect of sound on the physical body, the voice, the healing power of music, rhythm, the mysticism of sound, vibration, the power of the word, and much more.

Physics and Music by Harvey White and Donald White (Dover, 2014). A college textbook for students who want in-depth understanding to learn how musical sound is created and perceived. It surveys a wide range of topics related to acoustics, the general principles of sound, the different ways in which sound can be generated, musical scales, harmonics, the characteristics of instruments, and much more.

The Power of Music by Elena Mannes (Walker, 2013). This text explores the power of music and its connection to the body, the brain, and the world of nature. It follows visionary researchers and accomplished musicians to the crossroads of science and culture to discover how much of our musicality is learned and how much is innate.

The Power of Sound by Joshua Leeds (Healing Arts Press, 2010). Leeds's book focuses more upon the importance of healthy auditory functions—the process of hearing—and how sounds can assist in learning, communication, and social interactions. In particular, it explores the subject of psychoacoustics, or how sound affects our nervous system, in depth.

The Roar of Silence by Don Campbell (Quest, 1989). This is an excellent book on toning and how the therapeutic power of sound is inherent in everyone. Breath, tone, and music are explored through meditations and exercises. Campbell guides us into the world of toning and chanting, awakening vibratory awareness by exploring the energy beneath sound.

The Secret Language of the Heart by Barry Goldstein (Hierophant, 2016). Barry is an award-winning composer and producer who shares how each of us—the musical and the nonmusical alike—can harness the power of music to dissolve creative blocks, reverse negative mind-sets and attitudes, alleviate specific illnesses and ailments, and improve overall health.

Self-Healing by Ranjie Singh (Health Psychology, 1997). Singh's book shows how stimulation of the pineal gland through self-created sound increases its production of melatonin and presents exercises to increase your melatonin production. Melatonin is a hormone that enhances sleep, promotes longevity, boosts the immune system, and may be a treatment for cancer.

Sound Healing for Beginners by Joshua Goldman and Alec W. Sims (Llewellyn, 2015). Despite its name, this book is an excellent guide for both neophytes and adepts in the field of sound healing, covering everything from the scientific and magical healing nature of sound to the five elements of sound. We highly recommend it.

Sound Medicine by Wayne Perry (Musikarma, 2005). This book is an excellent guide to healing with the human voice. It explores the natural harmonics within the voice in order to develop the natural therapeutic capabilities of creating overtones. It features many different techniques and exercises for using the voice for healing.

The Tao of Sound by Fabien Maman (Tama-Do, 2008). This book covers Maman's thirty-five years of pioneering work. It links the human body, organs, chakras, and subtle energy fields with the five elements of nature, eight directions of the Bagua, the Kabbalah, the stars, and beyond. It includes extraordinary photos that document the impact of acoustic sound on human cells.

This Is Your Brain on Music by Daniel Levitin (Penguin, 2007). A musician and a neuroscientist, Levitin has written a most interesting book which examines the connection between music and the brain. He looks at what happens when we listen to music and why we enjoy it so much.

Tone by Siegmund Levarie and Ernst Levy (Kent State, 1968). This book is a study of musical acoustics. It is not new, but gratefully, the information with regard to acoustics is still relevant and valid. Most books on this subject are complex, but this book is relatively easy to understand and contains great information on sound.

Toning: The Healing Power of the Voice by Laurel Elizabeth Keyes and Don Campbell (DeVorss, 2008). This easy-to-read book is the work that for many initiated the extraordinary path of using self-created sound for healing and transformation. It is considered a classic in the field of sound healing, and rightfully so. Don Campbell has added his commentary, making the material even more valid.

Words of Power by Brian and Esther Crowley (Llewelyn, 1990). A very usable manual on sound, this book focuses on mantras from cultures around the world that can be used to promote healing and higher states of consciousness. Of the many books on the subject, this is one of our favorites.

Books on Belief, Quantum Physics, and Prayer

Biology of Belief by Bruce Lipton (Hay House, 2016). This ground-breaking work by Dr. Lipton in the field of new biology will forever change how you think about thinking. Lipton unveils stunning new discoveries about the interaction between your mind and body and the processes by which cells receive information.

The Intention Experiment by Lynne McTaggart (Simon & Schuster, 2007). This book investigates the science of intention through exploring various cutting-edge research and laboratory work on the subject. The book also provides great information on our relationship with the vast quantum energy field that surrounds and connects each of us.

The Isaiah Effect by Gregg Braden (Hay House, 2001). Braden is a dear friend as well as being a wonderful writer, researcher, and purveyor of ancient wisdom. In this book he decodes the lost science of prayer and prophecy, exploring the technology of a lost mode of prayer and presenting a dazzling new interpretation of the key prophecy from the Dead Sea Scrolls.

Neville Goddard: The Complete Reader by Neville Goddard (Audio Enlightenment, 2013). Neville, an American spiritual teacher who was born in the early 1900s, wrote a series of short books on various aspects of spirituality that have influenced many of our greatest new thought teachers. This book is a collection of all ten of his spiritual classics.

The Power of Intention by Wayne W. Dyer (Hay House, 2005). This book explores intention as a force in the universe that allows the act of creation to take place. Dr. Dyer explores intention on many levels, offering specific ways to apply these principles in daily life.

Stalking the Wild Pendulum by Itzhak Bentov (Destiny Books, 1988). This is an extraordinary book by a groundbreaking scientist. It presents new perspectives on the limitless possibilities of human consciousness, showing us that we are part of an expanded, conscious, holistic universe. It is clear and concise, focusing on many important aspects of vibrations and much more.

You Are the Placebo by Joe Dispenza (Hay House, 2015). Dr. Dispenza shares scientific evidence about the power of the placebo effect, with numerous documented cases of its role in reversing cancer, heart disease, depression, crippling arthritis, and Parkinson's disease. The book concludes with a meditation for changing beliefs and perceptions.

Books on Breath and Yoga

The Breath of Life: Integral Yoga Pranayama by Swami Satchidananda (Integral Yoga, 2015). Swami Satchidananda, one of our beloved Hindu teachers, has created a step-by-step instructional program in pranayama, the yogic breathing practices. It offers detailed guidance on how to incorporate these most powerful of healing practices into your daily routine for physical and mental purification and centering. It is suitable for complete beginners as well as more advanced students.

Conscious Breathing by Gay Hendricks (Bantam, 1995). This book draws on many years of research and practice to present a simple yet comprehensive program that can be used every day to improve energy, mental clarity, and physical health. As the essential life-force of the body, the breath influences how we feel on every level—emotional, mental, and physical.

Kundalini: Yoga for the West by Swami Sivananda Radha (Shambhala, 1978). This book focuses on the chakras from the classic Hindu tradition, along with the *bija* mantras and how they can be utilized to assist the forces of evolution.

The Practice of Nada Yoga by Baird Hersey (Inner Traditions, 2013). This book sheds light on nada yoga, the yoga of sound and, in particular, listening. Nada yoga is rooted in the Rig Veda, one of the world's oldest religious scriptures. It is full of information and exercises to help readers learn how to listen more intimately with their ears, hearts, and minds.

Pranayama: The Breath of Yoga by Gregor Maehle (Kaivalya, 2012).

This is one of the most comprehensive books on pranayama, the yogic science of breathing. It addresses both the Eastern spiritual aspects of this subject as well as the Western scientific focus, including the effects of pranayama on the nervous system. The book teaches many different techniques of pranayama for healing and spiritual transformation.

The Yoga of Breath by Richard Rosen (Shambhala, 2002). This book guides the reader in learning the basics of pranayama and using them in existing yoga practices. There are step-by-step instructions on experiencing breath and body awareness. Rosen also includes the history and philosophy of pranayama, presenting practical suggestions on how to utilize the various techniques presented in the book.

Books on Alternative Vibrational Healing

The Body Electric by Robert O. Becker and Gary Selden (William Morrow, 1998). This fascinating text tells the story of our bioelectric selves. It includes information on the use of electricity in the field of regeneration and the healing process and explores new pathways in our understanding of evolution, acupuncture, psychic phenomena, and physical rejuvenation.

Energy Healing by Ann Marie Chiasson (Sounds True, 2013). Dr. Chiasson has studied various alternative energy-healing techniques with masters from many different traditions, including Vedic, Chinese, and shamanic. The book begins with theoretical information, providing an understanding of why energy medicine works. It then offers many practices that readers can use to energetically heal themselves.

Energy Medicine by Donna Eden (Jeremy P. Tarcher, 1999). This book includes information on the chakras, the meridian system of acupuncture, and much more. There is material on how these different systems relate to health, illness, and pain. It is considered a classic in the field of energy medicine and is recommended for people interested in alternative healing.

Hands of Light by Barbara Ann Brennan (Bantam, 1988). This book has presented information on subtle energy medicine and bioenergetics healing for many decades. It includes material that focuses on the chakras and the subtle body and how they connect to an individual's health and wellness. Barbara offers techniques on a variety of subjects including seeing auras, understanding the human energy field, and expanding abilities for spiritual healing.

Perfect Health by Deepak Chopra (Three Rivers Press, 2001). Dr. Chopra is one of the most influential medical doctors to bring knowledge of Ayurvedic medicine and alternative healing to the West. This is a practical guide to harnessing the healing power of the mind, including a step-by-step program of mind-body medicine tailored to individual needs.

Vibrational Medicine by Richard Gerber (Bantam, 1992). Dr. Gerber explores the benefits of many different therapies that utilize vibratory healing, including homeopathy, acupuncture, color and light healing, and other therapies. One of the original books on the topic, it has been recently updated to include material on sound.

Music

We have found only a few recordings that utilize the hum, along with elongated vowel sounds. We have also included in this list some recordings that readers may find of particular interest with regard to the therapeutic and transformational nature of music.

Music by Jonathan Goldman

Ascension Harmonics (2009). This album, winner of 2009 COVR Visionary Award, was designed to help awaken listeners through enhancing altered states of consciousness and heightened awareness. With overtone chanting, Tibetan bowls, and bells, these undulating waves of sound assist vibrational activation and frequency shifts. This recording is excellent for enhancing deep states of meditation, shamanic journeys, and the ascension process.

Chakra Chants (1999). This recording is the 2000 winner of the COVR Visionary Award for both the Best Healing and Meditation Album as well as Album of the Year. It combines the sacred vowels, Pythagorean tuning forks, elemental and shabd yoga sounds, male and female choral voices, and much more, and it is designed for meditation and deep sound healing.

Cosmic Hum (2012). This recording features the sounds of thousands of people humming together to emulate the original sound of manifestation, with an undulating flow of sonics to induce powerful altered states of consciousness and deep relaxation. It includes cymatic frequencies to enhance health, binaural brain-wave frequencies for amplifying the human energy field, and Tibetan bowls.

The Divine Name (2005). Working with spiritual scientist Gregg Braden, Jonathan released this extraordinary CD that allows you to experience the sacred power of God's personal name. Rediscovered by Jonathan after more than 2,300 years, the Divine Name is found within the DNA of all life. It is a sound, reproducible with the human voice, that has the ability to heal and transform.

Ultimate Om (2004). This album contains the sound of the "rolling *Om*," a continuous tone created by a roomful of people chanting the *Om* mantra. To many who hear it, it sounds like a slowly evolving hum with flutes weaving in and out of the mix. These flute sounds are actually vocal overtones. The overall sound creates a gentle but profound spiritual listening experience.

Music by Others

Ascension Codes by Tom Kenyon (2011). This recording provides sonic codes that bring the listener to higher levels of being. Kenyon has a beautiful voice that he uses to create wonderful layers of vocal harmony to bring peace and tranquillity. His intention is to raise the consciousness of the listener and to bring forth healing energies from other dimensions.

Current Circulation by David Hykes and the Harmonic Choir (1992). With this recording, the singers create new melodies and chords by simultaneously shifting both the harmonic and fundamental notes, sometimes in converging directions, or by holding the high harmonic while varying the fundamental. The choral vocal work is very relaxing and beautiful—it's great for meditation.

Healing Bees: Creation by Valerie Solheim (2014). This recording features the sounds of a healthy beehive. Dr. Solheim believes that when one listens to the sounds of a healthy beehive, we are listening to the sounds of a super organism—a living unified field. She suggests that these sounds can enhance health and heighten spiritual awareness.

Hearing Solar Winds by David Hykes and the Harmonic Choir (1982). This music is very beautiful and transformative. It features gorgeous choral voices creating vocal harmonics. Together Hykes and his choir build chords based upon the harmonics in each other's tones and create Pythagorean tuned chords. The result is cloud-like in its sound and very hypnotic. It's an amazing recording that relaxes and enhances meditation.

Hu Chanting by Michal Hadam (2014). *Hu* (pronounced like the word "you") is considered in many traditions to be the sound of the Divine. This recording features Hadam doing an hour-long *hu,* multitracked so that it sounds like one continuous undulating wave of extended sound that is soothing and meditative. It sounds very much like a hum or an *Om*.

Lightship by Tom Kenyon (2014). This is a powerful psychoacoustic tool for exploring inner states of awareness and other realms of consciousness. The vocal patterns create powerful pulsating acoustic vibrations. The purpose of this recording is to lead the listener into direct contact with the remarkable worlds that reside within.

Spirit Come by Christian Bollmann (1991). Solo and group overtone singing by the Dusseldorf Overtone Choir with instruments such as the monochord, Tibetan bowls, and conch shells create a beautifully textured journey into sacred sound. This recording is excellent for deep relaxation and meditation. These lush sonic choral vocals embody that aspect of sacred sound that can truly transform.

Take Me As I Am by Christian Bollmann (2011). For over 25 years, Bollman and the Dusseldorf Overtone Choir have presented various recordings of overtone and choral singing. This recording features a composite of some of their very best sounds. The dynamic improvisations represent lush, sacred music from around the world, including India, Greece, and Hawaii.

Tibetan Master Chants by Lama Tashi (2006). We mentioned the Tibetan deep voice in chapter 5, and thus we feel it is appropriate to list this album by one of the great masters of this style of music. Nominated for a 2006 Grammy Award in the category of World Music, this recording features sacred chants from the Tibetan tradition in the extraordinary vocal register of the deep voice.

Tibetan Tantric Choir by the Gyuto monks (1987). This tantric college is perhaps most well known for being masters of the Tibetan deep voice. Their recording is composed of two nearly half-hour-long pieces that honor two Tibetan deities. The Gyuto monks have many other recordings available, but we feel that this early recording is sonically and vibrationally the best.

About the Authors

Jonathan Goldman, M.A., is an internationally renowned writer, musician, and teacher. He is an authority on sound healing and a pioneer in the field of harmonics. Jonathan is the author of several books, including his *The Divine Name,* winner of a Coalition of Visionary Resources (COVR) Visionary Award for Best Alternative Book in 2000, along with *The 7 Secrets of Sound Healing, Healing Sounds,* and *Shifting Frequencies.* A Grammy nominee, his award-winning recordings include *Chakra Chants, The Divine Name, Merkaba of Sound,* and *Reiki Chants.* He is the founder and director of the Sound Healers Association and CEO of Spirit Music. In 2011 Jonathan was named by Watkins' *Mind Body Spirit* magazine as one of the 100 Most Spiritually Influential Living People on the Planet. That year he was also inducted into the American Massage Therapy Association's Hall of Fame.

Andi Goldman, M.A., L.P.C., is a licensed psychotherapist specializing in holistic counseling and sound therapy. She is the director of the Healing Sounds seminars and codirector of the Sound Healers Association. She is a musician, teacher, sound healer, award-winning author, and the wife and partner of Jonathan Goldman.

Jonathan and Andi coauthored *Chakra Frequencies,* 2005 winner of the Coalition of Visionary Resources Visionary Award for Best Alternative Health Book.

Together, Jonathan and Andi have dedicated their lives to the path of service, helping to awaken and empower others with the ability of sound to heal and transform. They live in Boulder, Colorado. For more information, visit their website: **www.healingsounds.com**.

Index